Colonial Classics
Woodworking projects from the original 13 colonies

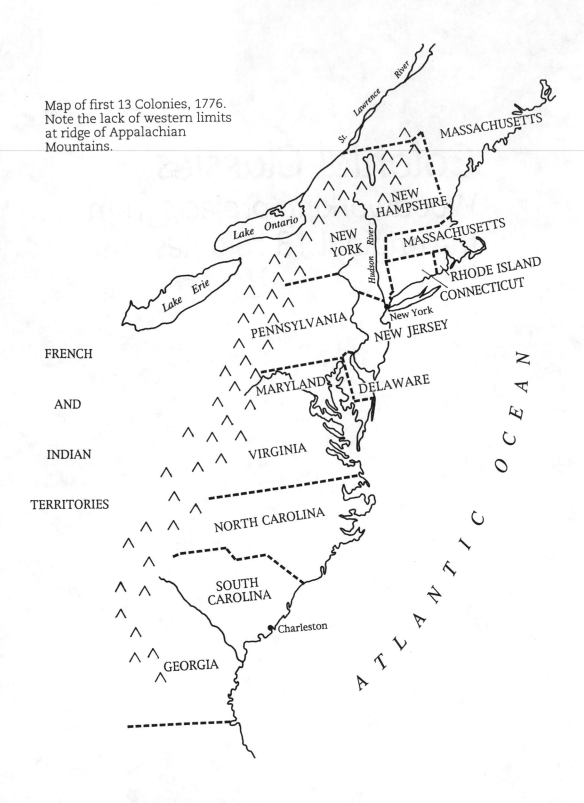

Map of first 13 Colonies, 1776. Note the lack of western limits at ridge of Appalachian Mountains.

St. Lawrence River

MASSACHUSETTS

Lake Ontario

NEW HAMPSHIRE

NEW YORK

Hudson River

MASSACHUSETTS

Lake Erie

RHODE ISLAND
CONNECTICUT

PENNSYLVANIA

New York

NEW JERSEY

FRENCH

AND

MARYLAND

DELAWARE

INDIAN

VIRGINIA

A T L A N T I C   O C E A N

TERRITORIES

NORTH CAROLINA

SOUTH CAROLINA

Charleston

GEORGIA

Colonial Classics
Woodworking projects from the original 13 colonies

Gloria Saberin

TAB Books
Division of McGraw-Hill, Inc.
Blue Ridge Summit, PA 17294-0850

FIRST EDITION
FIRST PRINTING

©1993 by **TAB Books**.
TAB Books is a division of McGraw-Hill, Inc.

Printed in the United States of America. All rights reserved. The publisher takes no responsibility for the use of any of the materials or methods described in this book, nor for the products thereof.

Library of Congress Cataloging-in-Publication Data

Saberin, Gloria.
   Colonial classics : woodworking projects from the original 13
colonies / by Gloria Saberin.
      p.   cm.
   Includes index.
   ISBN 0-8306-4197-1
   1. Furniture making.   2. Woodwork.   3. Furniture, Colonial—United
States. I. Title.
TT194.S23 1993
749.214—dc20   93-8050
                                                                      CIP

Acquisitions editor: Stacy Varavvas Pomeroy
Editorial team: April D. Nolan, Editor
               Joanne M. Slike, Executive Editor
Production team: Katherine G. Brown, Director
               Wendy L. Small, Layout
               Ollie Harmon, Coding
               Kristine D. Lively-Helman, Indexer
               N. Nadine McFarland, Quality Control
Design team: Jaclyn J. Boone, Designer
             Brian Allison, Associate Designer
Cover design: Paul Saberin, Farm Out Graphics, Chambersburg, Pa.
Cover photograph: Renfrew Museum & Park, Waynesboro, Pa
Special thanks for granting permission to feature special items: Hagley Museum and Library, Wilmington, Delaware; and Mystic Seaport Museum, Mystic, Connecticut.
Photography: Paul C. Saberin and Susan McCarl
Illustrations and plans: Paul C. Saberin   HT1

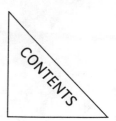

Small accessories

Furniture

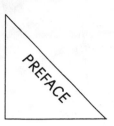

THE EASTERN SEABOARD HAS BEEN HOME TO MY family for many generations. Like my parents, I was born in Delaware, but our earliest ancestors came to this country from England, Sweden, France, and the Netherlands in the 1600s and settled in Delaware, New Jersey, New York, Pennsylvania, and North Carolina. I have traveled through all the 13 original states and have lived in Massachusetts, New York, Maryland, Delaware, Virginia, and Pennsylvania. I feel very much a product of the historical heritage of this coastal region.

I now live in rural Pennsylvania in a 200-year-old log home that is furnished with a collection of inherited antiques and reproductions I have made. Although I have all the modern conveniences, I feel very close to the settlers who once struggled to be self-sufficient here in these remote woods.

My love of woodworking and antiques combined with my family heritage inspired me to research this book, which is a collection of patterns for my favorite country pieces. Some are primitives; others are more sophisticated and complex. All are examples of the type of furnishings the early settlers made, used, and passed down to be cherished and copied by many successive generations.

Acknowledgments

I would like to thank several people whose expertise and assistance made *Colonial Classics* possible. Debra Hughes of the Hagley Museum, Wilmington, Delaware; Philip L. Budlong of Mystic Seaport Museum, Mystic, Connecticut; and the Victor DeLeons of Annapolis, Maryland, all enabled me to feature furniture from their collections.

Vaughan C. Chambers made the beautiful reproduction of the office shelves and helped me develop some of the plans.

S. Shane McCarl photographed many of the projects reproduced in black and white.

The illustrations and drawings are the work of my husband, Paul C. Saberin, whose help and encouragement were indispensable.

I greatly appreciate the patience of Bonnie Brechbill for her help in preparing the manuscript.

Finally, I am most indebted to the creative craftsmen of the thirteen colonies who produced the originals presented in the following pages. They settled and survived in this new land, and left us a wonderful heritage of the pieces they crafted so caringly.

THIS BOOK IS FOR ANYONE WHO ENJOYS WORKING with wood and has a love of American colonial antiques. If you have average experience with hand tools and simple power tools, you can make reproductions of early country pieces by following the patterns included here. These simple, functional projects are typical of furnishings made by farmers and itinerant craftsmen who lived in the early colonies of the Eastern Seaboard.

The antiques from which these patterns were derived were made by simple craftsmen who used indigenous woods in their attempts to duplicate sophisticated English and European furniture. The results were simplified versions of the pieces they copied. Other rustic pieces were created as practical solutions to fit a particular need in this rough, new land. All of these early American pieces were unpretentious and functional. Most were created on the farm where they were needed.

In this collection, I have included primitive and rustic pieces, as well as more elegant, complex ones. Start by making the Shaker sewing steps or the wall file, and then progress to the more complex projects, such as the pie safe. Following in the footsteps of our country's early settlers is challenging and fun. Craft as much as possible by hand, and you will learn much about how early American furnishings were first produced.

The original prototypes for these patterns are in museums, private collections, and in my own home. Even though you may find new and different uses for your reproductions, they will be as appealing and as useful as the originals.

Take care in choosing your wood, making the templates, and enlarging and laying out the pattern. Then proceed at your own pace, and you will produce an heirloom for your family to cherish. If you have any questions about tools and methods, I recommend using the *Woodworkers' Illustrated Benchtop Reference* by Spence and Griffiths, TAB 3177.

I hope the patterns in this book will encourage you to pursue woodworking in the tradition of our forefathers. Making reproductions of the pieces they made will bring much of our colonial history to life.

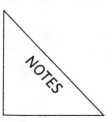

Notes for the woodworker

THE PROJECTS IN THIS BOOK are reproductions of furniture and accessories that were made by this country's earliest settlers, who could use only native woods and homemade tools. It is possible to make all of these projects with hand tools and some basic woodworking experience, but do not hesitate to use a band saw, scroll saw, drill press, router, or lathe if you have the skill to use them. Early craftsmen used the best tools available to them, and we should, too.

Even if you use power tools, you can achieve a desirable, authentic-antique look by keeping a hands-on approach to each project. Hand-finish your work, doing the sanding and scraping by hand. Use wooden plugs to cover countersunk screws, and avoid obvious shortcuts, such as using purchased dovetailing attachments. It is far better to change the plans and eliminate dovetails completely than to make factory-style, evenly spaced ones. The inherent irregularity provided by the use of hand tools will give your finished reproduction a more genuine look.

Some of the photographs in this book show the original antiques in their present setting. Other photos are of my reproductions, none of which are artificially aged or antiqued in any way. When you finish your own work, you might want to distress or antique it so that it will fit in with your authentic antiques.

Wherever possible throughout the book, I have provided plans for curving areas. The curved sections are gridded, and I have indicated the size to which the grid squares must be enlarged before you transfer them to the wood stock. The method I use is to lay out a grid of desired size on a large sheet of paper. Number and grid the coordinates on both the small grid in the

Patterns

book and on your larger grid. Then transfer the coordinate points to the large grid. Next, using a French curve, connect the points. Check the configuration several times as you proceed.

An easy way to enlarge plans is to use a photocopy machine with enlarging capabilities. (You can find these at most commercial printing companies or at a local copying center.) First, copy the pattern at book size. Then enlarge the pattern until the grid squares are the required size for a full-sized pattern. I like this method because I can make several copies of the full-sized pattern to use later. For very large pieces, you might have to cut and paste together several sheets of the enlarged copy.

Once you have a full-sized pattern, you need to transfer it to the wood. One way is to use carbon paper, but I often rub a soft pencil on the back of the pattern and then trace onto the wood. Another method is to cut a template of cardboard from the pattern and trace around it to transfer the design to the wood stock. This works well when you need to fit several pieces on the board around knotholes and other imperfections. One of my octogenarian friends, Harry Davis, always glues the paper pattern directly to the wood and cuts through paper and wood at the same time. This solution is perfect for the intricate patterns he cuts.

Wood

The pleasure of working with wood increases as you do more and more of it. A well-sanded or well-turned piece is as satisfying to the hand as it is to the eye. When a beautiful section of wood is crafted into an appropriate project, it is a joy to make and a pleasure to use.

It is not necessary to use fine wood for everything you make. As you work with different kinds of wood, you will learn how they can be used to best advantage. The first step in making a project is to determine which qualities of wood are necessary to its successful construction. Ask yourself: Does the project require wood with strength, fine grain, beauty, and color? Should it be easy to carve and/or turn? The characteristics of woods provided here will serve as a guide as you plan your initial selections.

Working Characteristics
of Woods Common to Colonial America

Wood	Strength	Texture	Other properties
Basswood	weak	fine	Easy to carve with knife or hand tools; fine grain; light, even color.
Birch	strong	fine to medium	Hard to work, but good for turning; fine grain.
Cherry	strong	fine to medium	Medium to work, good for turning, handles, furniture; beautiful, often reddish color.
Hickory	strong	medium to coarse	Easy to work when green; good for chairs, etc. Good for splitting when green.
Maple	strong	fine	Difficult to work by hand, but often beautiful and excellent for furniture.
Pines	soft to medium	fine to coarse; choose carefully	Relatively easy to work, good for nailing. Varies according to type of pine; some types are good for carving, but weak; others are stronger and good for simple furniture, toys, etc. Can have large, loose knotholes in some boards. Light color.
Poplar	medium	fine	Easy to work, fine texture, yellow to greenish color.
Walnut	strong	medium	Medium to work, rich color, even grain. Good for turning and nailing. Excellent for small pieces and furniture.

How you intend to finish your project also affects your selection of wood. A painted piece does not require the beautiful wood that a stained piece does. If you choose your wood carefully—according to the item you are making, the tools you have, and your ability—your woodworking will give you successful results and much pleasure.

When purchasing lumber for your project, allow enough for squaring off the ends and avoiding knotholes and imperfections—as well as for making a few mistakes.

Most of the materials lists give the exact measurements for the finished piece of wood. When a 1-inch board is indicated, it means a board that measures 1 full inch after being dressed or surfaced on both sides. Some of the thicknesses required might be difficult to find in ordinary lumber yards. Wood today is usually cut thinner than was the custom in colonial times. If you cannot locate the thickness of wood specified, you might have to order it custom-cut and planed.

When a project requires a large width of wood, such as for a tabletop, join together several pieces of the desired stock by gluing and blind-doweling edge to edge. If you are doing this yourself, you need large furniture pipe clamps and a method of making the edges perfectly straight before joining. Alternate the direction of the end curve in adjacent pieces in order to lessen the chance of the board twisting and curving out of shape after you join it into one large section.

Occasionally, building-supply houses sell wood that is already joined into large sheets. Take advantage of these oversized boards when you can. When I go to lumberyards, supply houses, or auctions, I carry a metal measuring tape and a list of the wood I need for future projects. Farm auctions are a good place to find old, full-cut lumber and pieces for tabletops. However, when you cut such old boards, be careful to avoid buried nails and parts of hinges that could damage your saw blade.

When you purchase your wood, pick it out yourself. Check carefully for straightness, and avoid large blemishes, roughness, and loose knotholes. After you have completed a few projects, you will develop a feel for the kind of wood that makes up easily. Trust your eyes and your hands as they appraise the wood's surface. A salesperson who is also a woodworker can be a great help in steering you to suitable wood.

Look through bins of leftovers from custom-milling orders. Often I find just the pieces I need for a small project in some discard pile, which saves me the trouble of special-ordering a small amount of a certain size. If you do have to order lumber custom-cut or custom-planed, purchase enough for several projects at once. This will save both time and money because once set-up costs are included, a large order often costs only a little more than a small one.

Tools

You can make the projects in this book without a wood shop or complicated power tools. Many small items, such as the hanging file (project 8) or the sewing steps (project 10), are easy to fashion with a coping saw, an X-Acto knife set, and a hand drill.

Sometimes I make a small project or parts of a larger one while sitting outside or by the fireside. People often tell me they would like to make things of wood but feel they need a complete workshop before they can start. All you really need to begin is space, good ventilation, and a sturdy bench or table.

If you are just getting started at woodworking, buy some of the basic tools and add others when needed. I suggest starting with hand tools and an electric drill. Buy the best tools possible, and keep their edges sharp and their handles tight. My initial tool kit included the following:

- rip saw
- crosscut saw (10 teeth to 1 inch)
- coping saw
- keyhole saw
- dovetail saw
- 16-ounce claw hammer
- tack hammer
- wooden mallet

- pliers, regular and needlenose
- set of screwdrivers, regular and Phillips
- set of chisels
- brace and bits
- eggbeater drill
- rasps and files, straight and curved
- nail set
- doweling centers
- marking gauge
- awl
- jack plane
- metal measuring tape
- carpenters square
- level
- metal bench rule
- utility knife
- X-Acto knife set and blades
- clamps
- woodworking vise

Over the years, I have added some simple power tools, and I now have a table saw, a band saw, a scroll saw, a drill press, a router, two belt sanders, and a palm sander.

My power tools are mounted on portable work tables so I am able to move them around in the shop—and even outside, when the weather permits. It is fun to work outdoors, especially when you are sanding or cutting large amounts of wood. I enjoy woodworking in the fresh air, and I hope you will try it. If you move power tools outside, be certain you have heavy-duty extension cords, and arrange the cords so you will not trip over them.

Power tools require less strength on your part and make the work go much faster. Add these when you feel you really need them. If you would use a power tool only occasionally, it might be more prudent to borrow it or to have another craftsperson make that special section for you. When I need turning done, I often take the wood to a local woodworker who is an expert at the lathe. It is difficult to find beautiful, large wood that is suitable for turning, so I would rather have it cut by a master turner than risk ruining the piece by turning it myself.

When you purchase power tools, do not use them until you know how to do so correctly and safely. Be certain they are mounted securely on their stands and have safe electrical hookups.

Power tools are a helpful option in woodworking. If you are planning to make several of one item, they are almost essential, unless, like former president Jimmy Carter, you prefer the actual manual crafting of each piece. He follows the pioneer spirit closely, felling the trees and proceeding with fashioning his hickory chairs in the exact methods used by his Georgia forebears.

Safety

Safety is an important consideration when working with any kind of sharp implement, and especially when woodworking. With a few precautions, you can make woodworking as safe as any daily household task. Here are nine basic safety rules for your workshop.

1. Keep your floor clear of all debris.
2. Keep your floor dry to prevent shocks or slipping.
3. Don't wear loose, floppy clothing that can catch in your tools.
4. If your hair is long, keep it pulled back securely.
5. Wear safety glasses or a face shield.
6. Keep your tools sharp and the handles tight.
7. Unplug all power tools when you are not working with them or when you are servicing them in any way.
8. Don't use a power tool unless you know how to use it properly.
9. If you have to use an extension cord, use a heavy-duty cord with three prongs.

Finishing

After you complete the assembly of a project, you will be ready to proceed with finishing. Finishing is as important to the success of your work as is the construction process. A good, well-applied finish protects the wood from dirt, moisture, heat, and small abrasions, as well as enhances the appearance of the reproduction.

Some of my instructions include finishing suggestions. However, it is not my intention to instruct in finishing methods or to limit your choices. As long as you use a technique and product appropriate to the style and period of your reproduction, it will appear authentic.

The freedom to individualize a project by your choice of finish is one of the rewards of making it yourself. I have made many knife trays, and I've finished each one differently, depending on where it was to be used. Even though the piece is a reproduction, you can make it truly your own creation by your choice of finish.

After you decide how you want your finished piece to look, consult an authoritative source and follow the instructions exactly. There are dozens of wood-finishing products available today, as well as many good books on the finishing techniques used in colonial America.

Preparing the surface

Whichever finishing method you select, proper surface preparation is essential. This includes sealing the wood, filling small defects, sanding, and staining if desired. This is perhaps the dullest part of the entire construction process, but it is vital if the finish is to enhance the completed piece.

After repairing any defects in the wood, start sanding. Use progressively finer grits of sandpaper, and wipe the project with a clean cloth between grits. If you want a weathered or rustic look to your reproduction, you might want to round the edges and distress the wood to simulate wear. I round the edges of my projects, but I prefer not to distress the surface. On fine-grained wood, I like to use wire wool or pumice for my final sanding. On some woods, you will want to apply a wood sealer. If you do, check the product's label to be sure it is chemically compatible with the coat you will use over it.

In all the surface preparation and applying of paints or varnishes, use high-quality brushes and rags. It is important to avoid brush marks, hairs, and lint, which might mar your finish. I find it necessary to do the finishing in an area removed from any woodworking. Either move your project out of the area, or refrain from sanding or cutting for a couple of days before you paint or varnish a piece.

Varnishing & staining

If the wood you have crafted is particularly beautiful, or if you wish to have it match other unpainted furniture in your home, I recommend using a clear finishing coat. When I specify varnish in this book I am using it as a generic term for any of the many protective finishes now on the market. I prefer the clear matte or satin finishes, which are similar in appearance to the old turpentine-based oil and wax finishes of colonial times.

Stain can be used to give different kinds of wood a more uniform appearance or to enhance the color of dull-looking woods. If you stain wood, be sure to wear lightweight plastic gloves to protect your hands. Stain is almost impossible to remove from around the fingernails.

I like to apply stains with a rag and wipe them off immediately with another cloth. Be sure to use a lint-free rag; you don't want lint stuck to the surface of your piece. Repeat the staining until you have the desired effect, and then let the piece dry overnight before proceeding with a top coat.

Painting

It would be sad to paint over walnut or birdseye maple, whereas a plain pine or basswood would be enhanced by a painted decoration. Be aware of the wood and its character as you plan the project. If you know you want a painted piece before constructing the project, choose your wood accordingly.

Painting techniques used during the American colonial period include sponge-painting, marbling, stenciling, wood-graining, and folk painting. Colonials used paints in mustard yellow, gray-green, gray- or teal-blue, and barn red. The Pennsylvania Dutch added very brightly colored designs to their furniture. Milk paints similar to the earliest ones are available again today; these would be suitable for almost all of the projects in this book.

Before you begin

Your project will go much more smoothly if you know what to expect and plan accordingly. To avoid unwanted interruptions or frustration, read and follow the guidelines provided here.

1. Study the drawings and read all accompanying text.

2. Make a complete list of the materials you will need, including all small items such as glue, nails, screws, plugs, hinges, sandpaper, etc. My materials lists do not always include all these small fasteners.

3. Determine which tools you will need to construct the project.

4. Buy everything you will need to complete the entire project.

5. Enlarge the pattern to working size, and cut any templates required.

6. If there are any complicated procedures, such as dovetails or mortises, cut a practice set on a scrap of the same wood you are using for the project. Be sure the grain is aligned in the same direction as on the pattern. Cut mortises about $\frac{1}{8}$ to $\frac{1}{4}$ inch deeper than tenons will need.

7. Transfer the pattern to the wood using a sharp pencil, a knife, or a scribe.

8. Cut out all the parts, and sand them well.

9. Make a trial assembly to make certain all parts fit together squarely and tightly.

10. Take the trial assembly apart, and reassemble the pieces with glue and fasteners, as needed.

11. You might want to stain or distress the wood at this time. If you want a slightly aged look, sand the edges at this time.

12. After the glue is completely dry, smooth it again with very fine sandpaper or steel wool.

13. Wipe the piece down with a lint-free cloth that has been slightly dampened with turpentine before starting the finishing process you have selected.

Small accessories

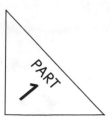

OFTEN, the early colonial homemaker lived in this undeveloped, rough country with only the barest of necessities. Although she used great ingenuity to create a home for her family, her choices were limited to very utilitarian items, usually made by a family member. Nonetheless, even everyday items were carefully designed and crafted. Fine craftsmanship was prized during colonial times, and men would often spend much time and effort to make a salt box, a slaw board, or another piece needed by the household. These handmade accessories were often the only decoration in a home, and they were cared for lovingly. Many women swept designs into their dirt floors in an attempt to beautify them, and I'm certain any special accessories in their homes were treasured by the entire family.

Although many of the projects in this section are for simple items, notice the special details that give them unique charm. The apron on the little stool, the curves of the salt box, the incisions and roundings on the wall file, and the wood graining on the office shelves are examples of the extra care and effort the early woodworker put into his work.

Make these projects adding color and details of your own, and you will create a family heirloom.

Towel rack

LONG BEFORE IT BECAME THE CUSTOM to fasten towel racks to the wall, colonials used standing towel racks in their bedrooms to hold their towels and coverlets. I discovered this antique in a coastal Rhode Island town where it had been in constant use. It has continued to hold guest towels in my home ever since. The rack has a delicate appearance, but is deceptively sturdy, having been in use for over 100 years. The legs were obviously carved, but it would be much easier to turn them on a lathe. The original antique had five layers of white paint and was probably painted right after it was made.

Materials

Hardwood

2 pieces legs (A)	1 × 1 × 29
2 pieces top supports (B)	1 × 1 × 6
2 pieces feet (C)	1 × 1 × 10¼
4 pieces rods (D)	½ × ½ × 23
4 pieces balls on feet (E)	1 × 1 × ½
4 pieces for attaching feet	¼ × ¼ × ¾

Miscellaneous
Glue
Sandpaper
Paint or varnish

You can follow the pattern as given or, by enlarging it slightly, make one to hold a quilt or a comforter. If you have more guest rooms than you have bathrooms, a rack such as this one will provide an easy solution for keeping towels and washcloths separated.

The measurements given here are for outside finished dimensions of blanks, and all dimensions are given in inches. You can substitute hardwood dowels instead of cutting the smaller pieces from boards. If you use doweling, it is possible to carve or sand the pieces to shape rather than turn them on a lathe.

Construction

1. Study the working drawing and the patterns to see how the carved sections fit together.

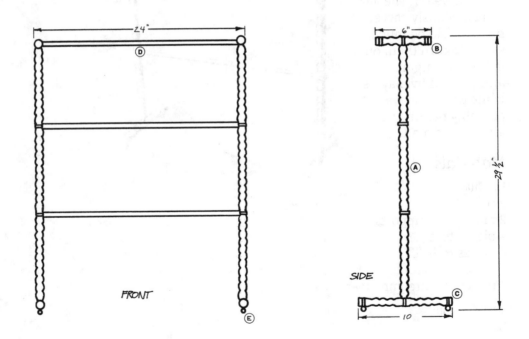

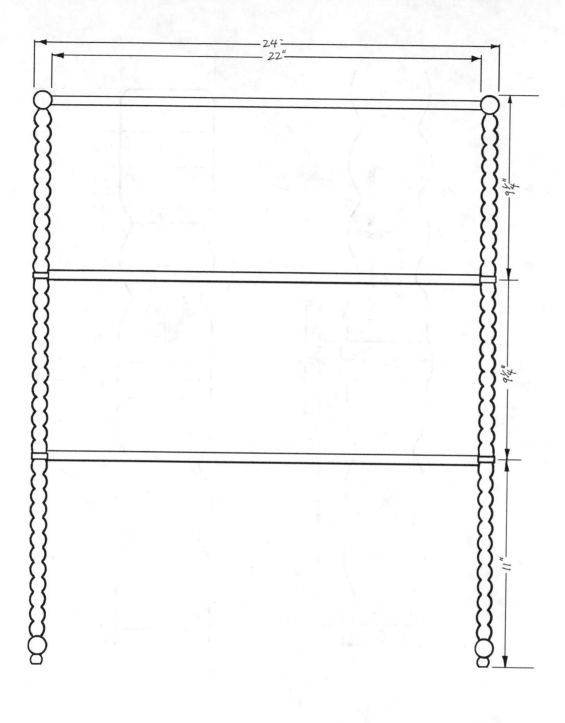

Towel rack 5

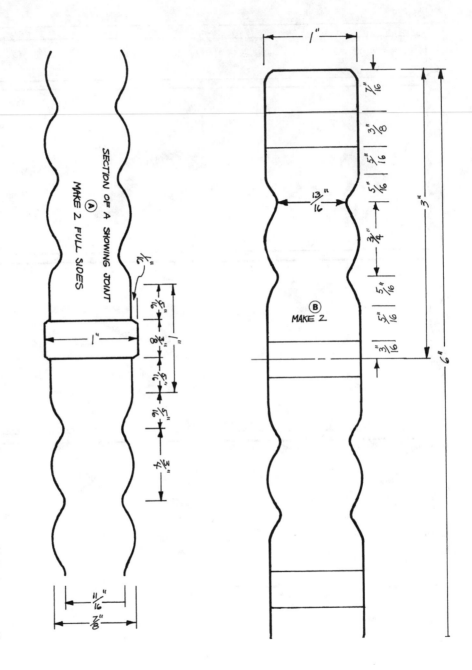

SECTION OF A SHOWING JOINT

Ⓐ MAKE 2 FULL SIDES

Ⓑ MAKE 2

2. Make a template for each of the carved sections, following the patterns shown on page 6 and below. Then, following these templates, carve or turn all pieces on the lathe, and sand well. Drill holes where indicated on pattern. Holes in As are ½" deep to hold rods D. Holes in C are ½" deep to hold As.

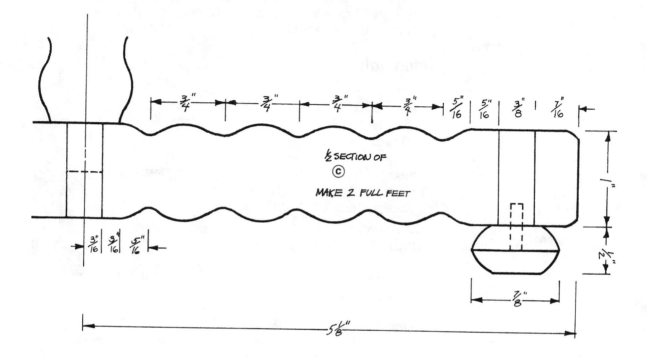

½ SECTION OF
Ⓒ

MAKE 2 FULL FEET

3. Make a trial assembly of both sides, the legs, the top supports, and the feet. When all parts fit neatly, glue and reassemble. Glue the wooden rods into the sides to complete the assembly. Sand thoroughly; then paint or varnish as desired.

Salt box

THIS TINY SALT BOX is on display in a South Carolina museum kitchen. It has a charming design and is easy to make. These wall boxes were used in most colonial kitchens to hold salt and other scarce spices.

Materials

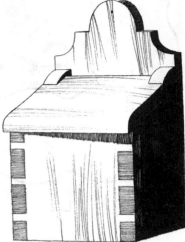

Wood

1 piece back (A)	$\frac{1}{2} \times 5\frac{5}{8} \times 8\frac{3}{4}$
1 piece front (B)	$\frac{5}{8} \times 4\frac{5}{8} \times 5\frac{5}{8}$
(This allows a little extra for tenons.)	
2 pieces sides (C)	$\frac{5}{8} \times 4\frac{1}{8} \times 6\frac{1}{2}$
1 piece lid (D)	$\frac{1}{2} \times 4\frac{1}{8} \times 5\frac{5}{8}$
1 piece bottom (E)	$\frac{5}{8} \times 3\frac{1}{2} \times 4\frac{5}{8}$

Miscellaneous
⅛ inch dowels or pins for joining
Glue
Sandpaper
Paint or varnish

Many of the early southern homes had their kitchens either in the high-ceilinged stone basement or in a separate building so that the family's food could be prepared without heating up the main house. In the humid, hot climate of the Carolinas, everything possible was done to keep the homes cool and dry. Homes of the prosperous and middle class alike were raised up on pillars and had large porches, overhanging roof lines, and shuttered windows. Even in the 1700s, southern landowners incorporated many architectural features designed specifically to make the homes comfortable during hot, humid weather. At the same time, the servants' homes were small, one-room cabins, more akin to the homes on the western frontier of our country.

The large, main houses were filled with furniture and accessories imported from Europe or made from patterns by cabinetmakers. The kitchens and other utility buildings contained small, more primitive items such as this salt box, which were made by a member of the household. This box is smaller than others I've seen, but is very decorative. I use mine to hold stamps and hang it near the door.

The measurements given in the materials list are for outside finished dimensions of blanks, and all dimensions are given in inches. As you can see, I have allowed a bit extra for the tenons and trim. Use clear walnut, pine, cherry, or other fine-grained wood.

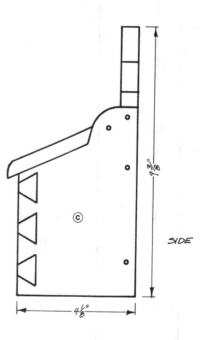

Construction

1. The illustration shows front and side view of the project. It is a good drawing to follow in assembly.

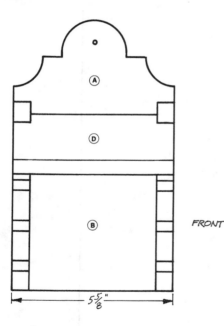

FRONT

SIDE

Salt box 9

2. Following the patterns on the next pages, cut out all blanks and sand them lightly.

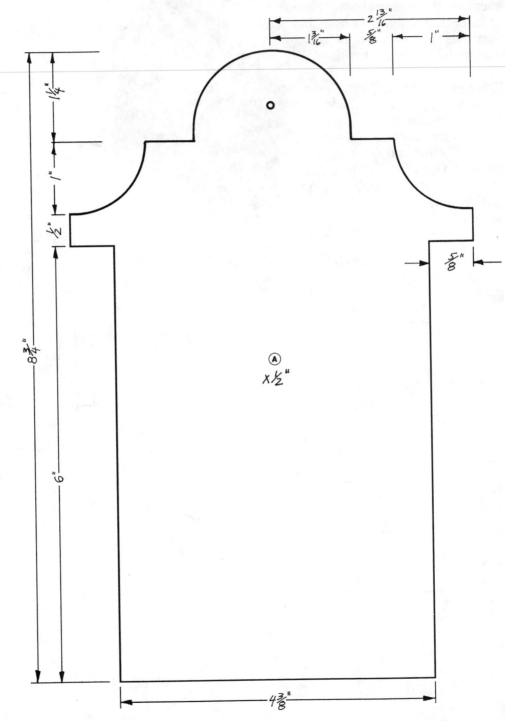

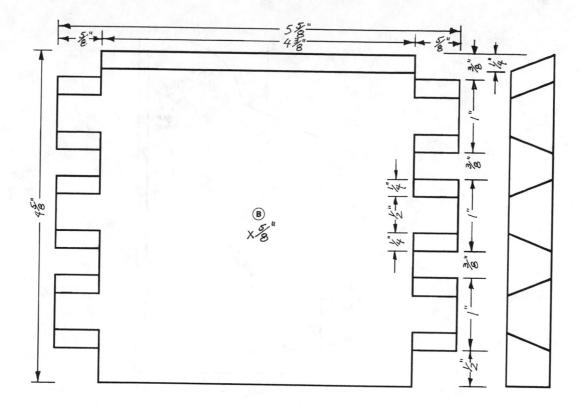

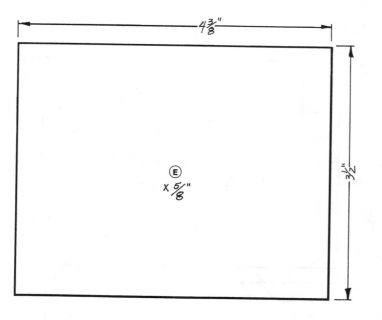

Salt box 11

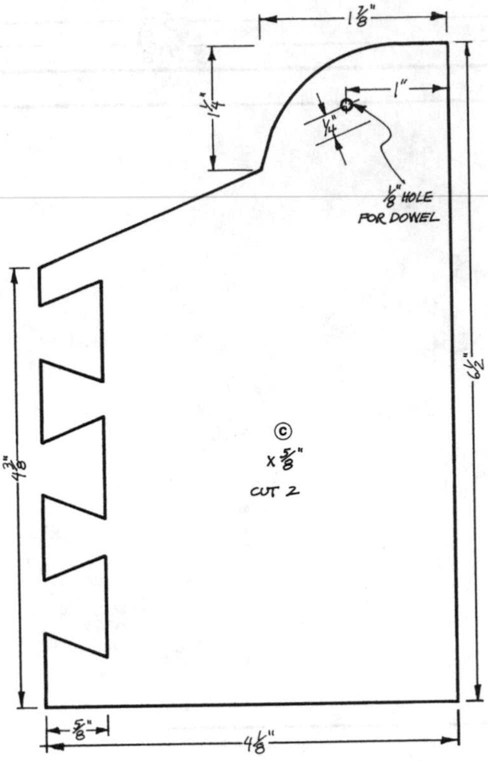
1 7/8"
1 1/4"
1"
1/4"
1/8" HOLE
FOR DOWEL
6 1/2"
4 3/8"
C
x 5/8"
CUT 2
5/8"
4 1/8"

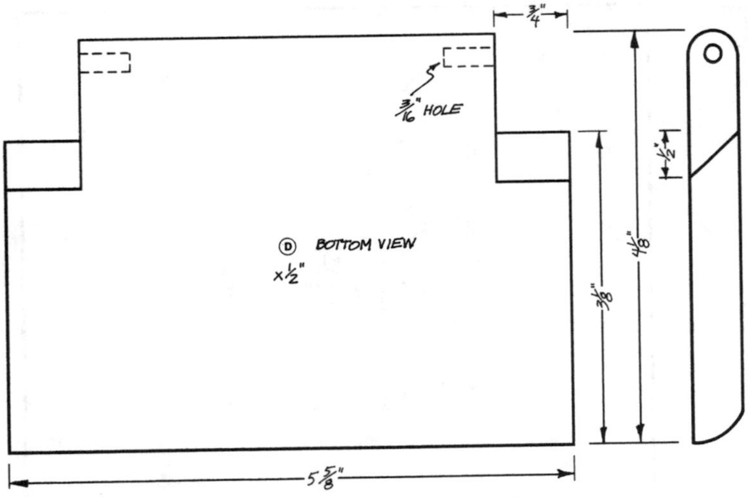
3/4"
3/16" HOLE
D BOTTOM VIEW
x 1/2"
1/2"
4 1/8"
3 1/8"
5 5/8"

3. Next, cut out dovetails in C, and drill holes for the lid hinges. Cut dovetails in B, leaving them slightly large, and then trim them carefully until they fit neatly into C. Sand lightly.

4. Glue and join B to Cs. Trim off dovetails where necessary. Fit A into place with dowels or a nail, if preferred. Set the box assembly over the bottom piece D, and pin or nail the bottom in place as shown in the pattern.

5. Next, cut the lid to shape, following the illustration. Trim and sand until the lid will move easily in place. Note drill holes in lid. They are larger than the holes in sides, which hold the dowels as hinges. Holding the lid in place, push ⅛-inch doweling through from outside of sides C into holes in lid. This should enable the lid to move up and down.

6. If you have used pine, you will probably want to paint the salt box. If you used a more interesting wood, stain and varnish the completed project.

PROJECT 3

Office shelf

THIS INTERESTING REPRODUCTION HAD ITS roots in Delaware, where the original is displayed in the Hagley Museum's original DuPont company office exhibit. It has two shelves and two drawers and might have held books and papers.

Materials

Wood

2 pieces sides (A)	¾ × 8½ × 38½
2 pieces shelves (B)	1 × 8½ × 21¾
1 piece middle shelf (C)	1 × 8 × 21¾
1 piece back of shelves (D)	½ × 11½ × 21¾
(Can be made by joining 2 pieces behind middle shelf)	
2 pieces drawer fronts (E)	1 × 5$\frac{5}{16}$ × 21¾
4 pieces drawer sides (F)	½ × 4$\frac{11}{16}$ × 7⅞
2 pieces drawer backs (G)	½ × 4$\frac{11}{16}$ × 21⅛
2 pieces bottoms (H)	¼ × 7⅛ × 20⅜

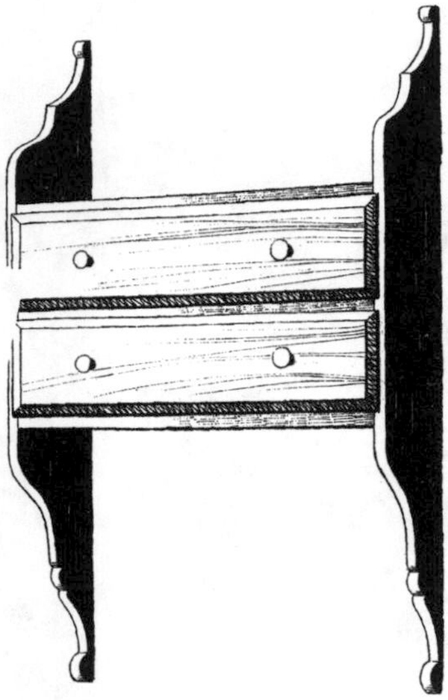

Miscellaneous

4 1"-diameter knobs, hardwood or porcelain
4 brass hangers
Sandpaper
Glue
Screws and plugs
Small nails to attach back and do drawers
Finishing coat

The prototype shelf was a donation to the museum and is dated to at least 1850 (it could be an even earlier piece). The surface is wood-grained, which was a technique used in early colonial times to make the local woods look more like the finer wood used in European furniture. I particularly like the scalloped curving design of the sides and the unique drawers that differ in width.

The original was obviously a one-of-a-kind piece made for a specific need. It is in quite good condition. I did not use wood-graining on the reproduction because I am not experienced in the technique, but if you want to try it, you can probably find good references in the library.

The wood you use can be pine, cherry, or maple for sides, shelves and front. My reproduction is of pine with a plywood back. Poplar can be used for back and bottom of drawers if desired.

The original was grain-painted, which you might want to try to duplicate. If not, pick out wood that has an interesting pattern, as was done on the reproduction shelf. NOTE: Measurements given in the materials list are for outside finished dimensions of blanks, and all dimensions are given in inches.

1. Study the working drawing on page 14 and the plan shown here. Following the patterns provided, cut out all blanks and sand them.

Construction

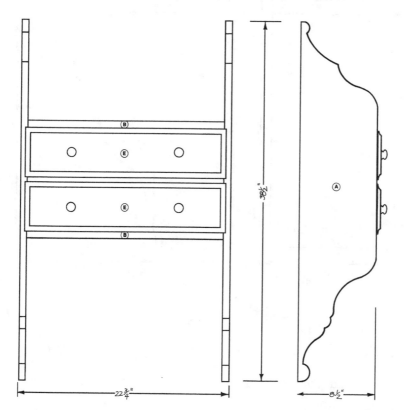

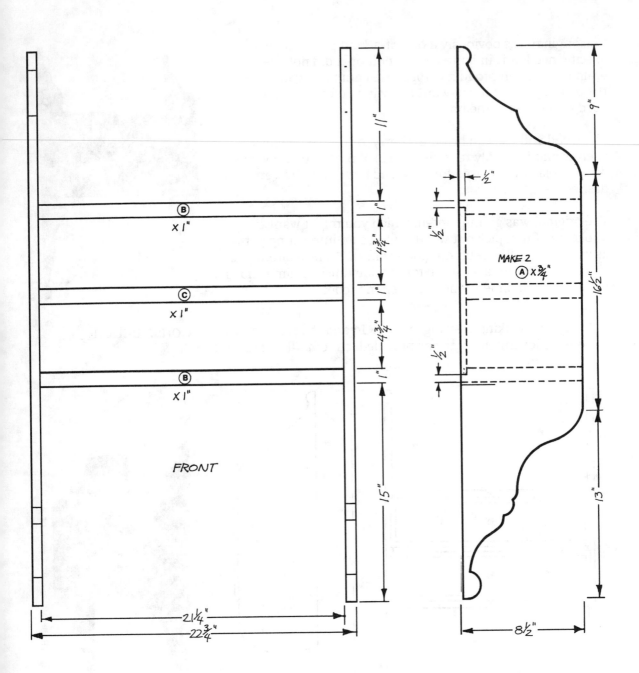

Ⓑ
X 1"

Ⓒ
X 1"

Ⓑ
X 1"

FRONT

11"

1"
4¾"
1"
4¾"
1"

15"

21¼"
22¾"

½"

½"

MAKE 2
Ⓐ X ¾"

½"

9"

16½"

13"

8½"

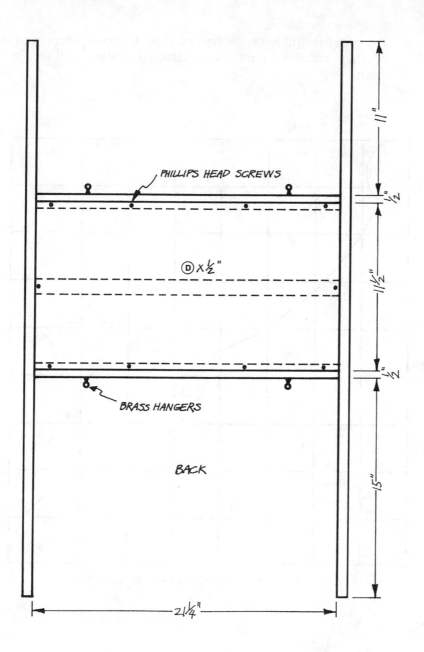

PHILLIPS HEAD SCREWS

Ⓓ X ½"

BRASS HANGERS

BACK

11"

½"

11½"

½"

15"

21¼"

Office shelf 17

2. Transfer the gridded scalloped patterns to the A pieces, and cut them out. Sand curves very thoroughly after cutting them.

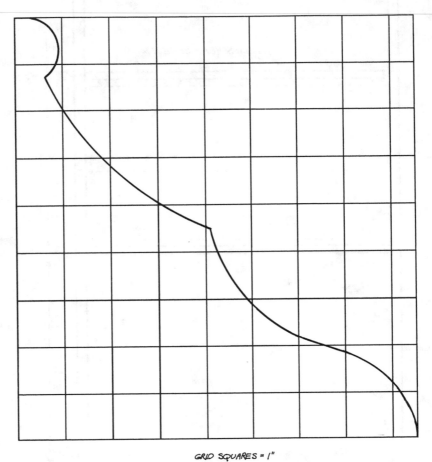

GRID SQUARES = 1"

3. Next, cut blind dados in the sides of the A pieces for the shelves to fit into. Rabbet ½" × ½" on the back of As for D. Also rabbet the back of shelves B. Then glue the shelves in place, and glue and nail D into place.

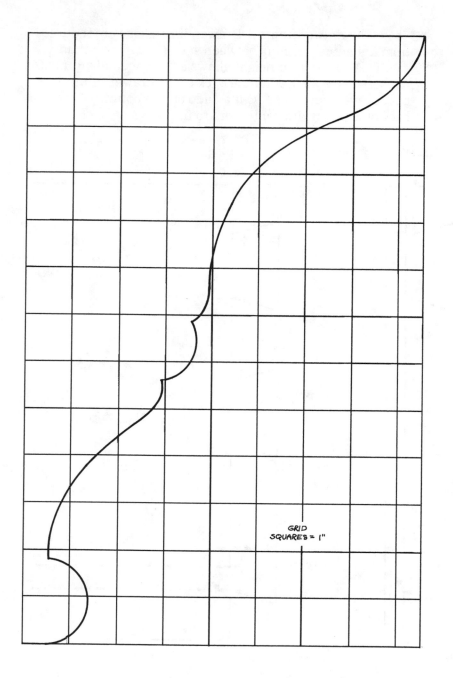

GRID
SQUARES = 1"

Office shelf 19

4. Shape the drawer fronts E. Drawer dimensions are reduced from the actual opening between shelves to allow for an easy fit. Drawer front height allows a 5⁄16" rabbet all around. Rabbet 5⁄16" × 1⁄2" all around the back of the drawer front. Then cut dovetails for sides F. Cut a dado on the bottom of the back of E for the drawer bottom to fit into.

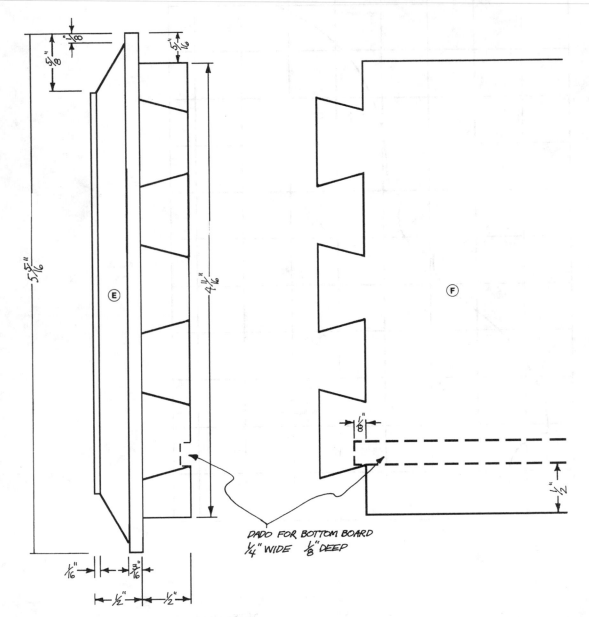

DADO FOR BOTTOM BOARD
1⁄4" WIDE   1⁄8" DEEP

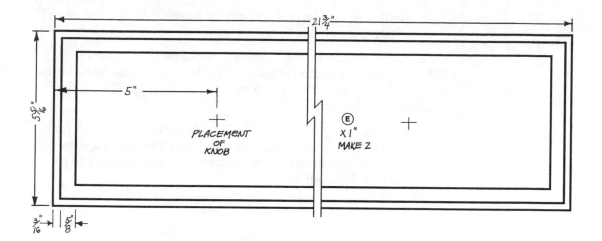

21¾"

5⅝₁₆"

5"

PLACEMENT
OF
KNOB

Ⓔ
X 1"
MAKE 2

3/16" 5/8"

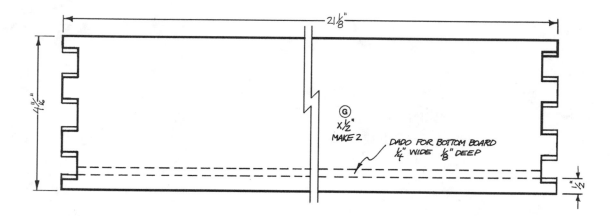

21⅛"

4¼₁₆"

Ⓖ
X ½"
MAKE 2

DADO FOR BOTTOM BOARD
¼" WIDE ⅛" DEEP

½"

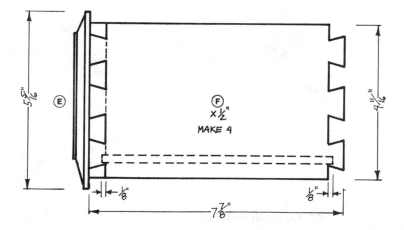

5⅝₁₆"

Ⓔ

Ⓕ
X ½"
MAKE 4

4¼₁₆"

⅛"

⅛"

7⅞"

5. Rout the raised panel on front of drawers E. You can chisel it instead, if you like.

6. Cut dovetails on the sides and backs of the drawers. Assemble the drawers with glue. Be sure to insert the bottom before adding the back. You can nail with small finishing nails if desired.

7. Resand the entire assembly. Finish with very fine sandpaper (150-grit or more). Add stains and finishing coats as desired, then add the knobs to the drawers and the hangers to the back of the shelf.

Little stool

THIS SMALL, LOW STOOL is from Georgia. It is a simple country piece and was probably made by a homeowner-craftsman for use by his own family. Early colonial Georgia encompassed a wide range of living conditions—from elegant plantations furnished with imported furniture to little slave homes sparsely furnished with simple, primitive pieces. This stool may have been used in many types of homes during its life time.

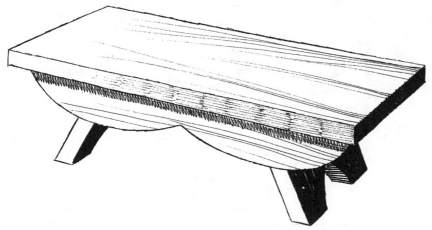

Materials

Wood
Use any good, clear wood, such as maple, cherry, poplar or pine.

1 piece for top (A)	¾ × 7½ × 16
2 pieces for aprons (B)	¾ × 2 × 15
2 pieces for legs (C)	¾ × 5½ × 5½

Miscellaneous
Glue
Sandpaper
Plugs to cover screws
Doweling or 1¼" screws

Perhaps used by a small child or as a foot stool by a young woman, it has probably served many purposes over the years. The paint on the original is badly worn now, but it still sits by the hearth in an historic Georgia home. The original is painted a dark teal-green, so I painted my reproduction in a similar shade.

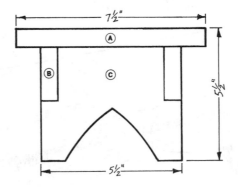

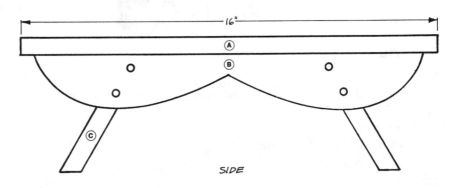

END

SIDE

Although it was originally made in the deep South, this stool will fit in wherever you choose to use it. Measurements given in the materials lists are for outside finished dimensions of blanks, and all dimensions are given in inches. Use any good, clear wood, such as maple, cherry, poplar, or pine.

1. Study the working drawing on page 23. Cut out the blanks for all pieces and sand them.

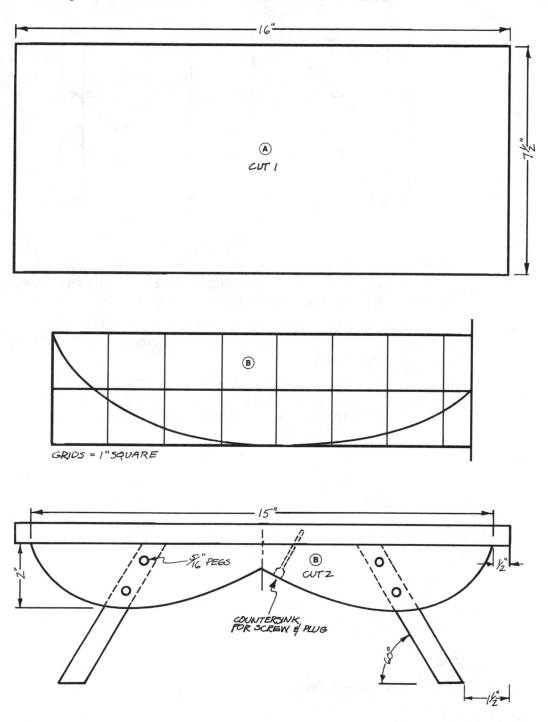

16"

7½"

Ⓐ
CUT 1

Ⓑ

GRIDS = 1" SQUARE

15"

2"

Ⓑ
CUT 2

5/16" PEGS

½"

COUNTERSINK
FOR SCREW & PLUG

60°

1½"

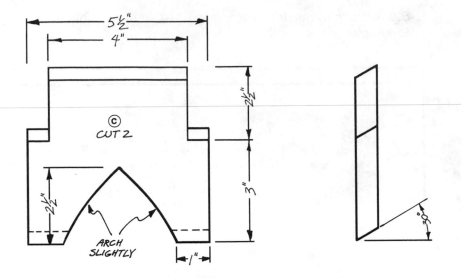

2. Following the plan above, bevel the legs. Then assemble the stool base, trimming carefully until it fits neatly and stands squarely. Check squareness with a level.

3. With a countersink bit, drill Bs to join legs C. Glue, then screw together Bs and Cs. Check squareness again, and trim if necessary.

4. Place top A upside-down on a bench, and glue the leg assembly to it. Drill holes in Bs, and screw the leg assembly to the top. Glue wood plugs over the screws, and sand. Paint or varnish as desired.

Shaving mirror

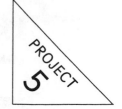
NORTH CAROLINA WAS THE HOME of this antique shaving mirror, but could have been from any of the prosperous homes of the colonial east coast. Although the original piece had wooden feet and knobs, these were replaced with metal legs and porcelain knobs, probably in the late 1800s.

Materials

Wood

Use cherry or walnut for sections that show, and pine or poplar for the drawer back and bottom.

2 pieces box bases (A)	$\frac{3}{8} \times 6 \times 15\frac{3}{4}$
(Only the top base has mortises cut in it.)	
1 piece back of box (B)	$\frac{3}{8} \times 2\frac{5}{8} \times 14\frac{3}{4}$
2 pieces sides of box (C)	$\frac{3}{8} \times 2\frac{5}{8} \times 5\frac{3}{4}$
1 piece drawer front (D)	$\frac{3}{8} \times 2\frac{5}{8} \times 14\frac{3}{4}$
1 piece drawer back (E)	$\frac{1}{4} \times 2\frac{1}{8} \times 14\frac{3}{4}$
2 pieces drawer sides(F)	$\frac{1}{4} \times 2\frac{1}{4} \times 5\frac{5}{8}$
1 piece drawer bottom (G)	$\frac{1}{4} \times 5\frac{1}{2} \times 14\frac{1}{4}$
2 pieces mirror support (H)	$\frac{3}{4} \times 1\frac{3}{8} \times 11\frac{13}{8}$
1 piece mirror back	$\frac{1}{8} \times 8\frac{5}{8} \times 10\frac{7}{8}$

$\frac{3}{16}$-inch dowel or metal pins to hold mirror

2 pieces rounded molding for making mirror frame	
(Use bought molding.)	$\frac{3}{4} \times \frac{3}{4} \times 11\frac{5}{8}$
2 pieces rounded molding (as above)	$\frac{3}{4} \times \frac{3}{4} \times 9\frac{1}{2}$

Miscellaneous

1 mirror, $8\frac{1}{2}$"×$10\frac{5}{8}$"
$\frac{3}{4}$" finishing nails
4 little hardwood feet
2 wooden or porcelain knobs
Brads for mounting mirror
Glue
Sandpaper
Stain and varnish

Made in cherry and finely crafted, this piece is as useful on a bureau or dressing table today as it was in its original home. North Carolina was settled mainly by English colonists from the north, and this shaving mirror might have been brought down with them or made in Carolina, copying an older, English-made piece. Many families in the colonies took small accessories with them as they moved, and other craftsmen made reproductions of European-made furnishings by following patterns that were bound in pamphlets and spread throughout the settlements.

By the time of the Revolutionary War, many homes of the more prosperous colonists contained rather elegant, decorative furnishings, compared to the roughly and sparsely furnished homes of the pioneers who settled the lands to the west of the Appalachians.

The measurements given for this project are for outside finished dimensions of blanks, and all dimensions are given in inches. Allow extra for tenons and trim after assembly. Use cherry or walnut for sections that show, and pine or poplar for the drawer back and bottom.

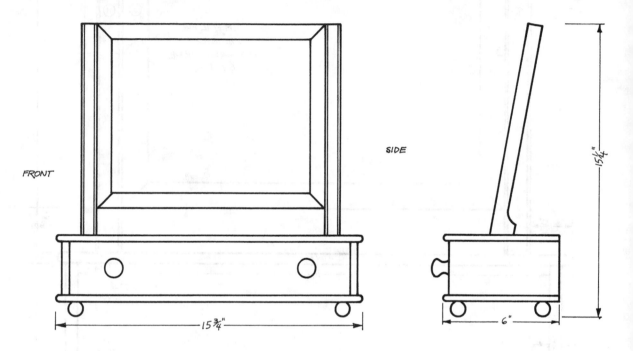

1. Study the working drawing on page 27. Cut out all the blanks, following the patterns on pages. Sand all the pieces, and round the edges of the A pieces. Cut mortises in the top of A, following the pattern on page 30.

2. Cut out the two H pieces. Trim the tenons so they fit neatly into mortises in top of A. Remove the H pieces from A, and set them aside. Assemble the main box, gluing and nailing with small finishing nails.

Construction

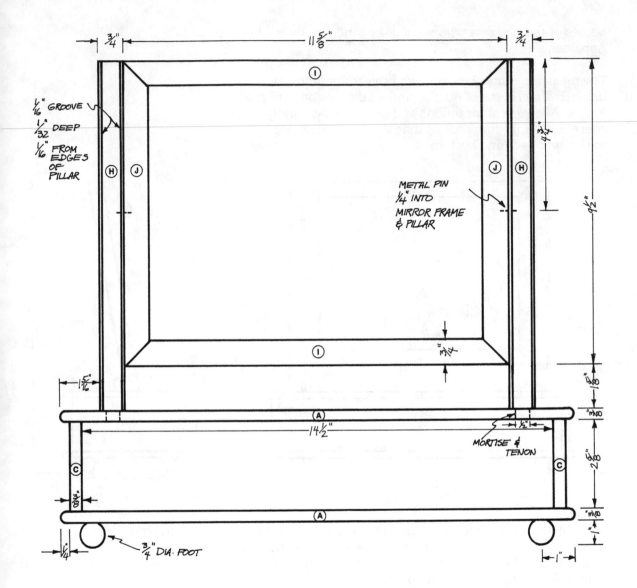

3/4"   11 5/8"   3/4"

I

1/16" GROOVE
1/32" DEEP
1/16" FROM
EDGES
OF
PILLAR

H   J

4 3/4"

9 1/2"

METAL PIN
1/4" INTO
MIRROR FRAME
& PILLAR

J   H

I

3/4"

1 5/16"

1 3/10"

A

14 1/2"

1 1/2"

MORTISE &
TENON

C   C

2 3/10"

3/8"

A   5 3/10"

1"

1 1/4"   3/4" DIA. FOOT   1"

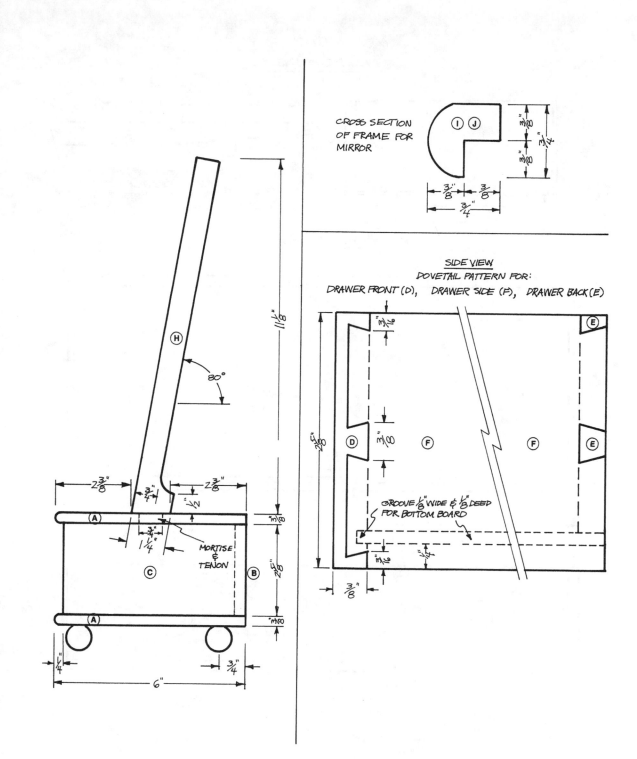

CROSS SECTION
OF FRAME FOR
MIRROR

$\frac{3}{8}$" $\frac{3}{4}$"
$\frac{3}{8}$"
$\frac{3}{8}$" $\frac{3}{8}$"
$\frac{3}{4}$"

I J

11$\frac{1}{8}$"

80°

H

2$\frac{3}{8}$" $\frac{3}{4}$"   2$\frac{3}{8}$"
$\frac{1}{2}$"

$\frac{3}{4}$"
1$\frac{1}{4}$"
MORTISE
&
TENON

A
C
B
A

$\frac{3}{80}$"
2$\frac{5}{8}$"
$\frac{3}{80}$"

$\frac{1}{4}$" $\frac{3}{4}$"

6"

SIDE VIEW
DOVETAIL PATTERN FOR:
DRAWER FRONT (D),   DRAWER SIDE (F),   DRAWER BACK (E)

$\frac{3}{16}$"

E

$\frac{3}{80}$"

D $\frac{3}{80}$"   F   F   E

GROOVE $\frac{1}{8}$" WIDE & $\frac{1}{8}$" DEEP
FOR BOTTOM BOARD

$\frac{3}{16}$" $\frac{1}{4}$"

$\frac{3}{8}$"

2$\frac{5}{8}$"

Shaving mirror 31

DRAWER ASSEMBLY

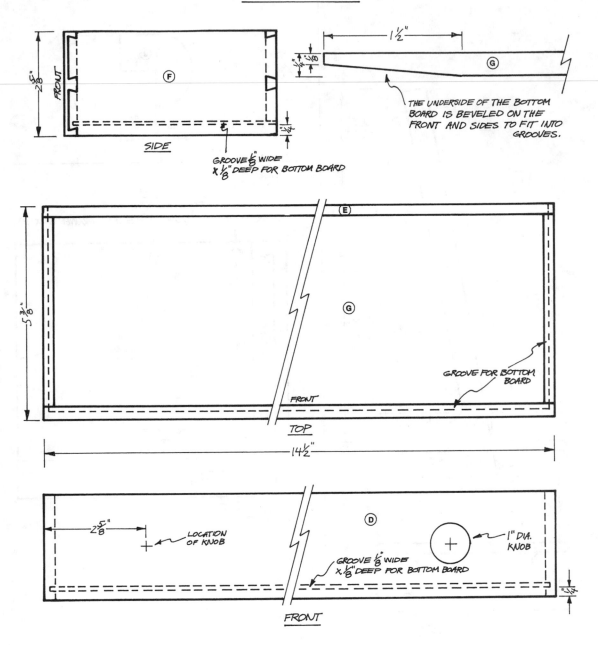

SIDE

GROOVE ⅛" WIDE
x ⅛" DEEP FOR BOTTOM BOARD

2 ⅝"

FRONT

THE UNDERSIDE OF THE BOTTOM
BOARD IS BEVELED ON THE
FRONT AND SIDES TO FIT INTO
GROOVES.

1 ½"

5 ⅜"

FRONT

GROOVE FOR BOTTOM
BOARD

TOP

14 ½"

2 ⅝"

LOCATION
OF KNOB

GROOVE ⅛" WIDE
x ⅛" DEEP FOR BOTTOM BOARD

1" DIA.
KNOB

FRONT

32 Colonial Classics

3. Cut blind dovetails and grooves in D, E, and F, as indicated on the plan on page 31, bottom right. When you have gotten the dovetails to fit neatly, glue drawer box together.

4. Bevel the bottom of G on three sides so it will fit into grooves in D and Fs. Then slide G into place, and secure it with small nails.

5. Mount the feet onto main box assembly.

6. Shape the wood for I and J, following the pattern on page 30. Miter the edges of I and J, and glue and nail them together. Stain and varnish all parts at this point.

7. Drill a ¼" hole through the H pieces and in the side of the mirror frame. Mount the mirror in the frame and back, securing it with brads. Mount the mirror section into the H pieces, and glue this into the top of A.

8. Mount knobs on the D drawer front, and put drawer in box.

Spice cabinet

THE EARLY SETTLERS in Massachusetts carried on a continuing trade by ship with England, Europe, and the West Indies. This ship traffic continued until modern times and enabled the people of the area to access many luxuries that were difficult for other colonies to obtain. Salt, tea, and spices were available in Massachusetts in early days, but they were expensive. The colonists valued spices highly, and many little multidrawered cabinets similar to this one have been a useful fixture in New England homes for several hundred years. The small drawers probably held all the spices a householder could afford to have at one time, or perhaps the rest were kept elsewhere, under lock and key.

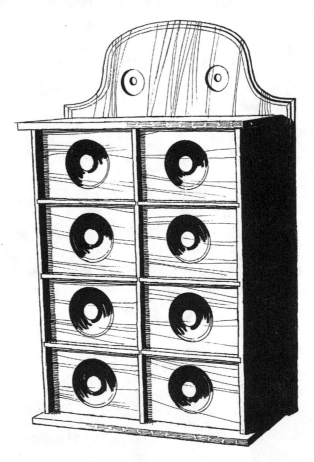

Wood
Use pine or maple for parts that show and pine for all other parts.

1 piece back (A)	⅜ × 10⅝ × 16¾
2 pieces top (B) & bottom (C)	⅜ × 4¾ × 9⅞
2 pieces sides (D)	⅜ × 4⅞ × 12
1 piece center (E)	⅜ × 4⅞ × 12¼
6 pieces dividers (F)	¼ × 4¼ × 4¼
2 pieces drawer fronts (G)	⅜ × 2⅞ × 4
6 pieces drawer fronts (H)	⅜ × 2¾ × 4
4 pieces drawer G sides (I)	⅜ × 2⅝ × 3⅝
12 pieces drawer H sides (J)	⅜ × 2½ × 3⅝
2 pieces drawer G backs (K)	¼ × 2⅝ × 4
6 pieces drawer H backs (L)	¼ × 2½ × 4
8 pieces drawer bottoms (M)	¼ × 3⅞ × 4

Miscellaneous
8 ½" knobs, porcelain or wood
Small nails, ¾" & ⅞"
Glue
Sandpaper
Stain and varnish

The original cabinet is from Massachusetts and has never been painted. Although it is an old, authentic style, it probably was made in the 1800s; I know it has been in my family over 75 years, and it was stained in the 1900s. Many of these cabinets were originally painted. I have seen some very old cabinets painted blue and mustard yellow.

Some old pieces have wooden or porcelain knobs on the drawers, but this one has handles carved out of the drawer fronts. If you prefer to make plain drawer fronts, add the knobs after the cabinet is completed. The measurements given in the materials list are for outside finished dimensions of blanks, and all dimensions are given in inches. Use pine or maple for parts that show and pine for all other parts.

Construction   1. Study the working drawing on page 34. Enlarge it, if necessary, to be sure you understand how the pieces go together. Cut out all blanks, following the patterns on the next pages. Cut grooves where indicated with chisel or router. Drill holes for hanging in back. If you plan to carve knobs in the drawer fronts instead of attaching knobs, carve them now.

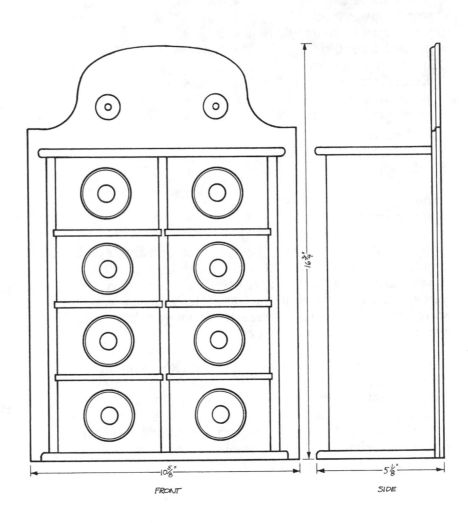

FRONT   SIDE

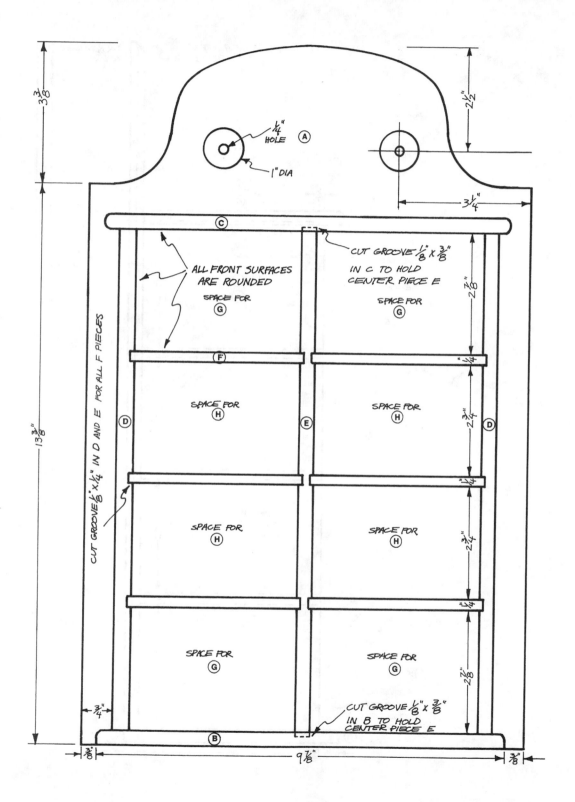

$3\frac{3}{8}$

$2\frac{1}{2}$"

$\frac{1}{4}$" HOLE Ⓐ

1" DIA

$3\frac{1}{4}$"

Ⓒ

CUT GROOVE $\frac{1}{8}$" X $\frac{3}{8}$" IN C TO HOLD CENTER PIECE E

ALL FRONT SURFACES ARE ROUNDED

SPACE FOR Ⓖ

SPACE FOR Ⓖ

$2\frac{7}{8}$"

Ⓕ

$\frac{1}{4}$"

CUT GROOVE $\frac{1}{8}$" X $\frac{1}{4}$" IN D AND E FOR ALL F PIECES

$13\frac{3}{8}$"

Ⓓ

SPACE FOR Ⓗ

Ⓔ

SPACE FOR Ⓗ

$2\frac{3}{4}$"

Ⓓ

$\frac{1}{4}$"

SPACE FOR Ⓗ

SPACE FOR Ⓗ

$2\frac{3}{4}$"

$\frac{1}{4}$"

SPACE FOR Ⓖ

SPACE FOR Ⓖ

$2\frac{7}{8}$"

CUT GROOVE $\frac{1}{8}$" X $\frac{3}{8}$" IN B TO HOLD CENTER PIECE E

$\frac{3}{4}$"

Ⓑ

$\frac{3}{8}$"

$9\frac{7}{8}$"

$\frac{3}{8}$"

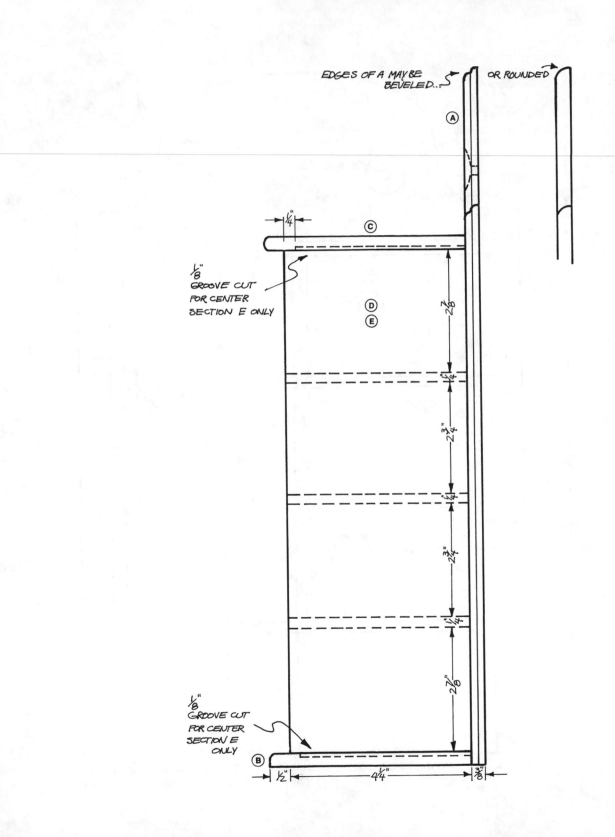

EDGES OF A MAY BE BEVELED...

OR ROUNDED

Ⓐ

¼"

Ⓒ

⅛"
GROOVE CUT
FOR CENTER
SECTION E ONLY

Ⓓ
Ⓔ

2⅞"

¼"

2¾"

¼"

3¼"

¼"

2⅞"

⅛"
GROOVE CUT
FOR CENTER
SECTION E
ONLY

Ⓑ

½"

4¼"

⅜"

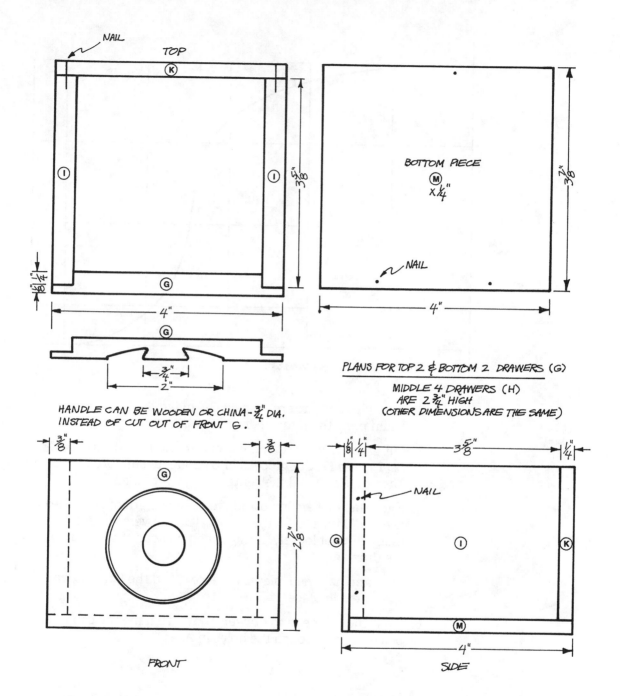

NAIL

TOP

Ⓚ

Ⓘ   Ⓘ

3⅝"

¼"
⅛"

Ⓖ

4"

Ⓖ

¾"
2"

HANDLE CAN BE WOODEN OR CHINA - ¾" DIA.
INSTEAD OF CUT OUT OF FRONT G.

BOTTOM PIECE
Ⓜ
X ¼"

3⅝"

NAIL

4"

PLANS FOR TOP 2 & BOTTOM 2 DRAWERS (G)

MIDDLE 4 DRAWERS (H)
ARE 2¾" HIGH
(OTHER DIMENSIONS ARE THE SAME)

⅜"   ⅜"

Ⓖ

2⅞"

FRONT

⅛" ¼"   3⅝"   ¼"

NAIL

Ⓖ   Ⓘ   Ⓚ

Ⓜ

4"

SIDE

Spice cabinet 39

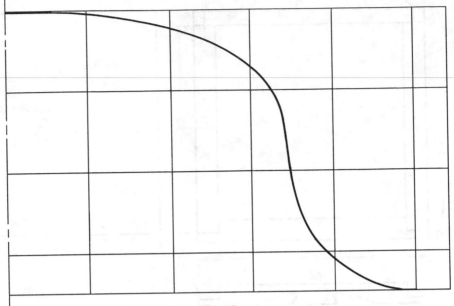

GRID SQUARES = 1"

2. Following the pattern on page 39, make the drawers, gluing and nailing them together.

3. Cut groove for E in C and B. Next, round the edges of B, C, Ds, Es, and Fs. Cut grooves in Ds and E to support shelves Fs. Then glue and nail the center piece E into C and B.

4. Place the drawers in position to check length of Fs. If they need adjustment, fix them now. The drawers should slide easily but not loosely. It might help to soap the bottom of the drawers.

5. Glue and nail the F pieces in place. Sand the F fronts, and glue them in place.

6. Stain the cabinet and drawer fronts. To hang the cabinet, place a rope through the holes in A.

Mailbox

THIS BOX FROM PENNSYLVANIA is very old and in excellent condition, despite being outside for a good portion of its life. Although intended for outside use, it was probably not used for mail. The words U.S. MAIL stenciled casually across the front were added many years ago, (see next page) but still long after the box was first constructed. The canvas hinge straps are also not original and might have replaced the earlier leather ones. I have tried to determine the box's original use but have not found an answer. It now hangs just outside our main entrance and is used to hold messages left by callers.

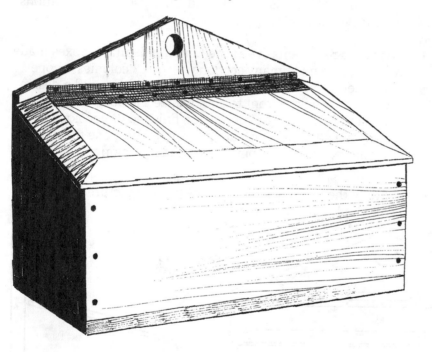

Wood
Use the wood of your choice; poplar and pine were used in the original.

Materials

1 piece back (A)	¾ ×10 × 14	
2 pieces side (B)	¾ × 6 × 6¾	
1 piece front (C)	¾ × 5 × 14	

| 1 piece bottom (D) | ⅝ × 7½ × 14 |
| 1 piece lid (E) | ⅝ × 7 × 14 |

Miscellaneous
Square-headed nails (or countersunk screws & plugs)
1½" × 12½" strip of heavy canvas tape or leather
Upholstery tacks
Glue
Sandpaper
Paint
Protective coat of weatherproofing varnish

I found the antique box at a Pennsylvania farm auction and happily added it to my collection of country antiques. Handmade and joined with old, cut nails, it has a rustic charm. The original paint was the barn-red color used for generations on Pennsylvania barns.

This box is representative of the homemade utility boxes made by homesteaders in many sections of our 13 colonies. I hope you will enjoy making one like this. You could stencil a design or your name on the front to personalize the box. Measurements given are for outside finished dimensions of blanks, and all dimensions are given in inches. Use the wood of your choice; poplar and pine were used in the original.

Construction

1. Study the working drawing and the plan pictured. Cut out all blanks, and sand.

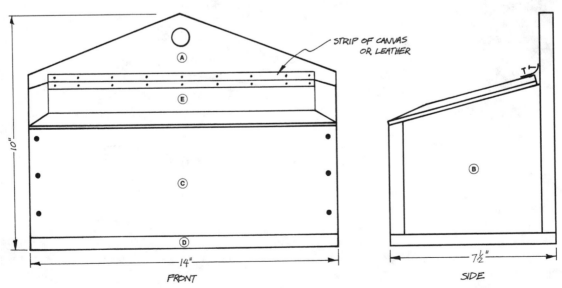

STRIP OF CANVAS OR LEATHER

FRONT

SIDE

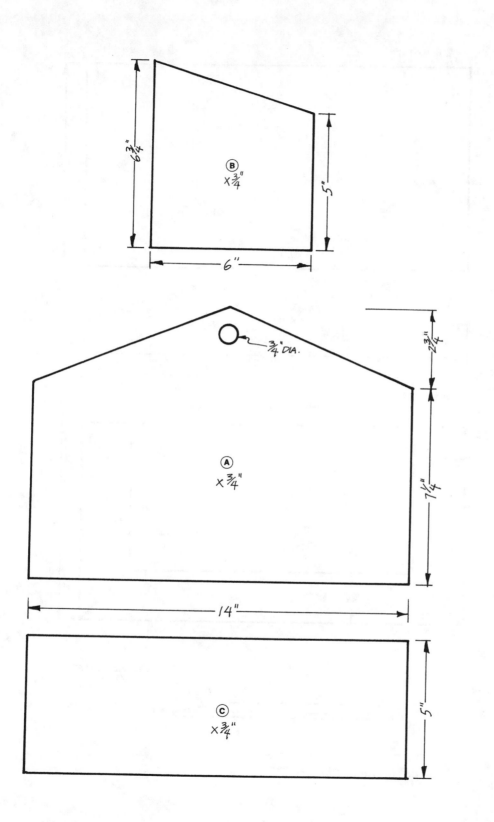

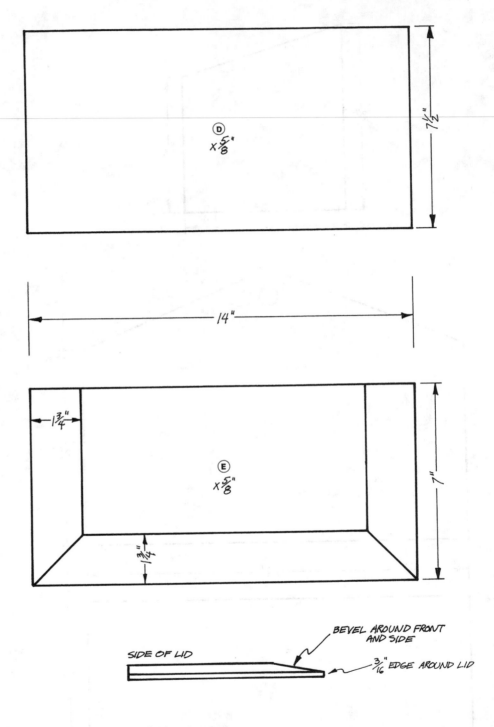

7½"

14"

⒟
X ⅝"

1¾"

7"

3¼"

SIDE OF LID

BEVEL AROUND FRONT
AND SIDE

⒠
X ⅝"

³⁄₁₆" EDGE AROUND LID

2. Drill a ¾" hole in A, as shown on pages 42 and 43. Following the pattern on page 44, bevel the three top edges of E.

3. Nail or screw the back to the sides, the front to the sides, and the bottom up onto the sides, back and front.

4. Paint the box and its lid now. The original box has U.S. MAIL stenciled on it. This was probably done years after it was first made, but nonetheless a long time ago. You may omit the stenciling completely, or stencil some other design or your name on the box.

5. Nail the canvas strip to the lid and then to the box. Leave about ¼" space along the back edge to enable the lid to move freely up and down when completed.

6. Seal the box with a weatherproofing varnish spray.

Hanging file

THE PROTOTYPE for this handmade wall file from New Jersey was perhaps made for an early office. Simple in design and sturdy in construction, it is well-suited for heavy-duty use. The only decoration consists of a few incised lines. Even in colonial times, items made for use in homes or offices were crafted with details intended to make them decorative as well as useful.

Materials

Wood
Use any clear wood; pine was used in the antique original
1 piece back (A)   ¾ × 10½ × 19¼
2 pieces sides (B)   ¾ × 6 × 14¾
2 pieces front (C)   ¾ × 3½ × 10½
2 pieces bottom (D)   ¾ × 6 × 9

Miscellaneous
1¼" hand-wrought or cut nails to fasten on front
Glue
Sandpaper
Screws and plugs or finishing nails to fasten other sections together
Stain, wax, or varnish

Since early New Jersey had many small businesses, I suspect that this piece was indeed made for commercial use as a file or an in-and-out box for a small office. I use the antique in my hall for separating incoming mail. Perhaps this was its original purpose.

The measurements given here are for outside finished dimensions of blanks, and all dimensions are given in inches. Use any clear wood; pine was used in the antique original.

Construction

1. Study the working drawing and the plan on page 46 to familiarize yourself with how the pieces fit together. Cut out all the blanks, following the patterns on the next pages and sand.

2. Incise grooves on Bs, as shown on page 48. Drill a ¼" hole in A for hanging the file.

3. Nail or screw and plug Cs, Ds, and A together. Then nail on the fronts.

4. Stain or varnish.

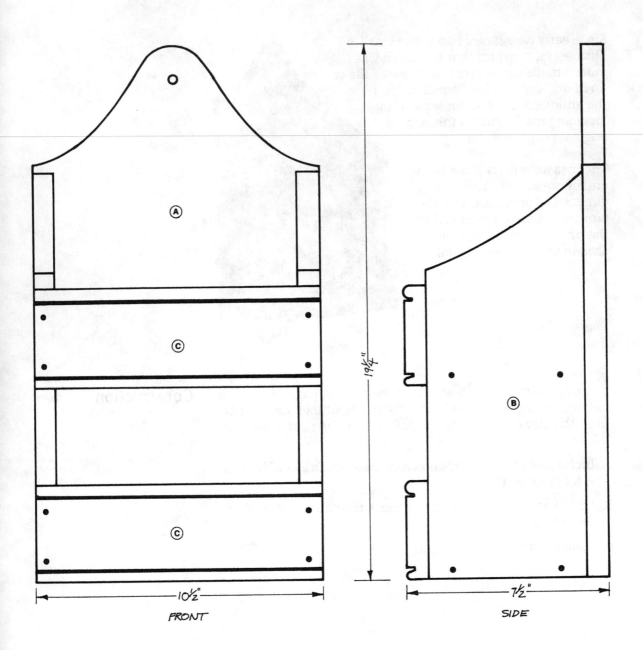

FRONT

SIDE

$10\frac{1}{2}$"

$7\frac{1}{2}$"

$19\frac{1}{4}$"

48 Colonial Classics

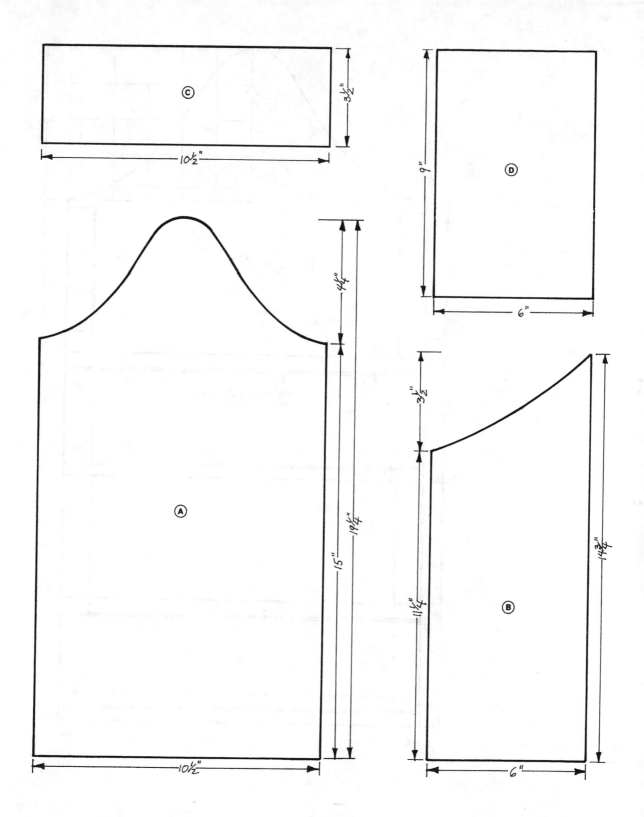

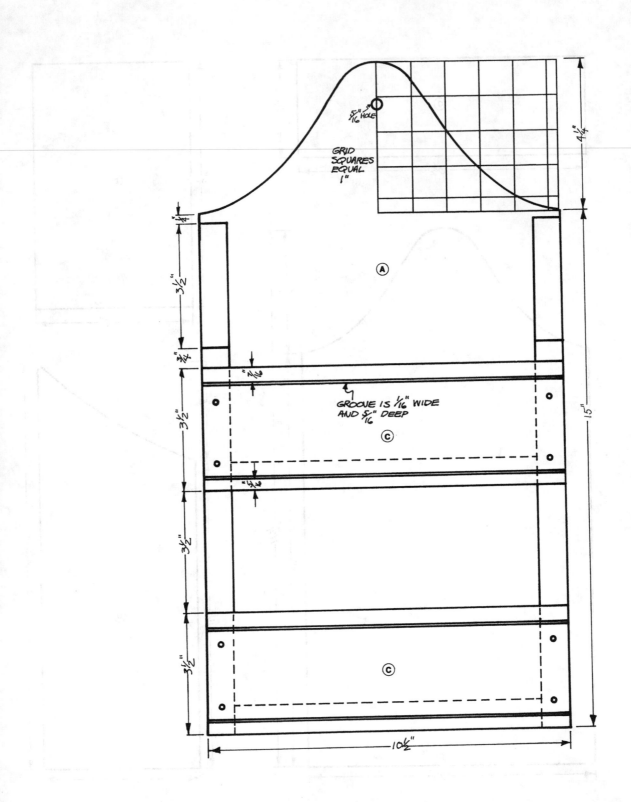

5"/16 HOLE

GRID
SQUARES
EQUAL
1"

4¼"

¼"

3½"

¾"
3"

A

1"/16

GROOVE IS 1/16" WIDE
AND 5"/16 DEEP

3½"

C

1"/16

3½"

15"

3½"

C

10½"

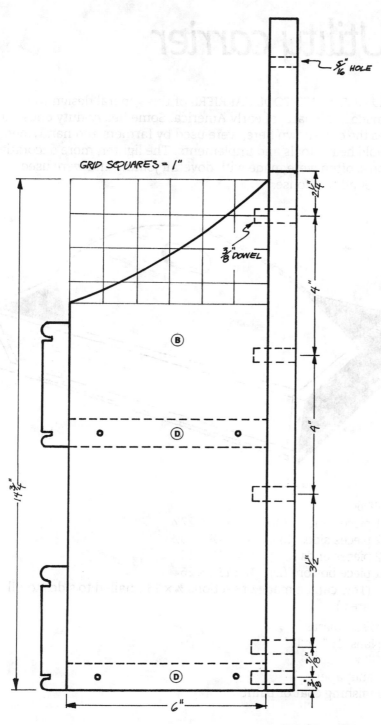

GRID SQUARES = 1"

$\frac{5}{16}"$ HOLE

$2\frac{1}{4}"$

$\frac{3}{8}"$ DOWEL

4"

B

4"

D

$3\frac{1}{2}"$

$14\frac{3}{4}"$

7/8"

$\frac{3}{8}"$

D

6"

Hanging file 51

Utility carrier

UTILITY AND TOOL CARRIERS of this general design were made in all parts of early America. Some heavy-duty ones, such as the one shown here, were used by farmers and handymen to hold heavy tools and implements. The lighter, more decorative ones often were made with dovetail joining and were used around the house.

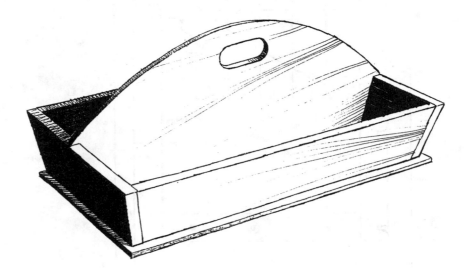

Materials

Wood
1 piece center (A)   ¾ × 11¼ × 27½
2 pieces sides (B)   ¾ × 4¾ × 26½
2 pieces ends (C)   ¾ × 4¾ × 15
1 piece bottom (D)   ¾ × 13½ × 26
   (This can be made of sections ¾ × 13½ nailed to sides to fill
   area.)

Miscellaneous
Nails, 1¼" or 1½"
Glue
Sandpaper
Finishing coat or paint

This particular carrier from Maryland is large and heavy and was perhaps used to carry items on a wagon rather than by hand. Some large carriers had canvas flaps nailed to the center board and these were used to cover objects in the side sections to keep them dry and clean.

This project is useful on a porch or in a hall to hold mittens, magazines, or other frequently used items. It could be mounted on legs to serve as a chair's side table.

The measurements given in the materials lists are for outside finished dimensions of blanks, and all dimensions are given in inches. Use any strong wood available to you for this project; appearance is not as important as strength.

1. Study the working drawing on page 52 and the plan below. Then cut out blanks, following the patterns on pages 54, and 55.

Construction

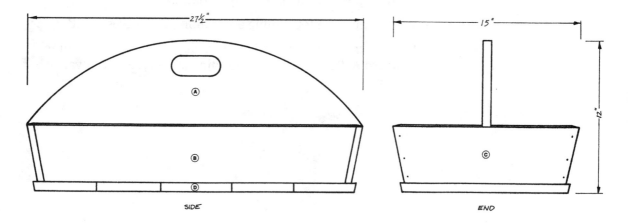

SIDE

END

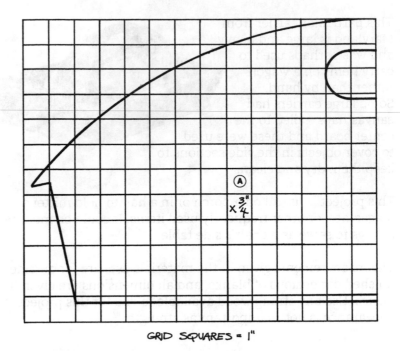

Ⓐ

$x \frac{3}{4}"$

GRID SQUARES = 1"

2. Cut grooves in ends C. Then cut the handle hole in A. Sand these pieces well, especially at handle hole.

3. Assemble the top, gluing and nailing the pieces together.

4. Form the bottom by nailing boards to sides and to center board A. Sand all edges, rounding slightly. Paint or varnish if desired.

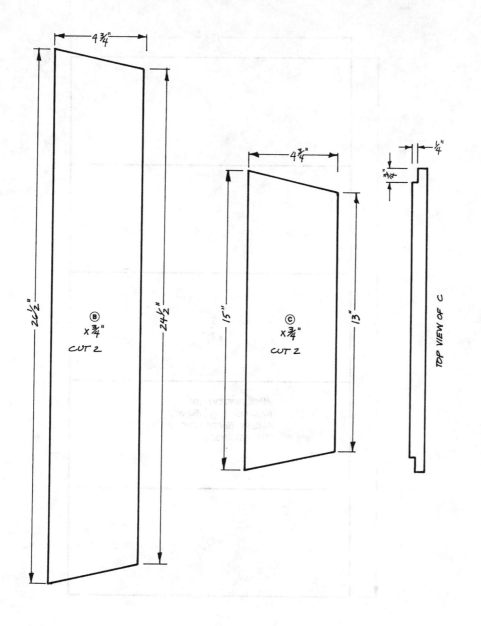

4 ¾"

26 ½"

B
x ¾"
CUT 2

24 ½"

4 ¾"

15"

C
x ¾"
CUT 2

13"

¼"

³⁄₈"

TOP VIEW OF C

Utility carrier 55

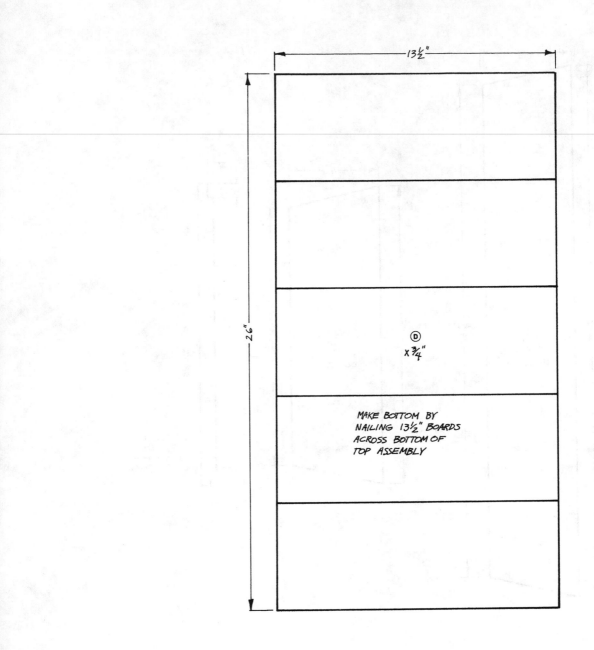

MAKE BOTTOM BY
NAILING 13½" BOARDS
ACROSS BOTTOM OF
TOP ASSEMBLY

Shaker sewing steps

PROJECT
10

THIS UNIQUE PROJECT is an adaptation of old Shaker sewing steps from New York. Although this piece looks like a small step stool, sewing steps actually were used as footrests by women when sitting for long periods of time. The seamstress or quilter could rest her legs by putting her feet in different positions on the steps. Many colonial women spent hours at a time working on their sewing and quilting, so these little stools received a lot of use.

Materials

Wood
2 pieces sides (A)   ¾ × 8 × 11
2 pieces steps (B)   ¾ × 5¾ × 14

Miscellaneous
8 1¼"-long flat-head screws
Doweling or plugs to cover screws
Glue

Sandpaper
Paint or other finishing coat

The Shakers came to New York state in 1774 in the midst of the colonial period in this country. Their many contributions to American life, especially in the area of fine design and woodworking, earn them mention in any discussion of early antiques. The Shakers invented the cut nail, the flat broom, and numerous other useful items. Their beautiful, simple designs are as contemporary and useful today as they were when first designed.

This pattern is easy to construct and can be used in many places around a home. I use mine to display some of my small collections or to hold a colorful arrangement of plants.

Measurements given are for outside finished dimensions of blanks, and all dimensions are given in inches. For this project, use wood of your choice. Use maple, cherry, or walnut if you want to oil or stain and varnish the piece; use pine or poplar if you are going to paint it.

Construction

1. Study the working drawing on page 56 and the plan on page 59 to see how the pieces fit together. Then cut out all the blanks and sand them.

2. Drill holes through the top of B into the sides A, using countersink drill bit. Sand the fronts and sides of the steps, rounding them slightly.

3. Glue and screw the steps to the sides. Then cut the plugs, and glue them in place over the screws.

4. Sand the entire assembly again. Finish as desired.

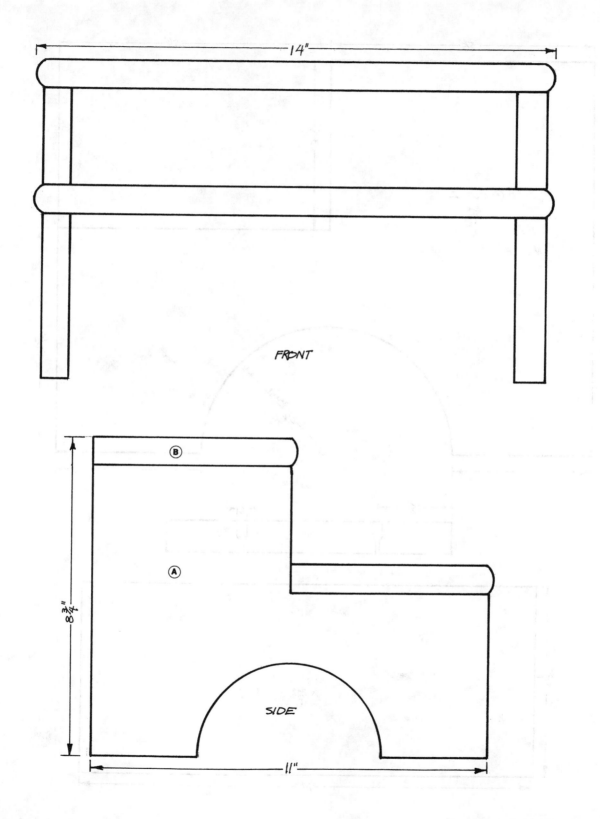

14"

FRONT

Ⓑ

Ⓐ

8¾"

SIDE

11"

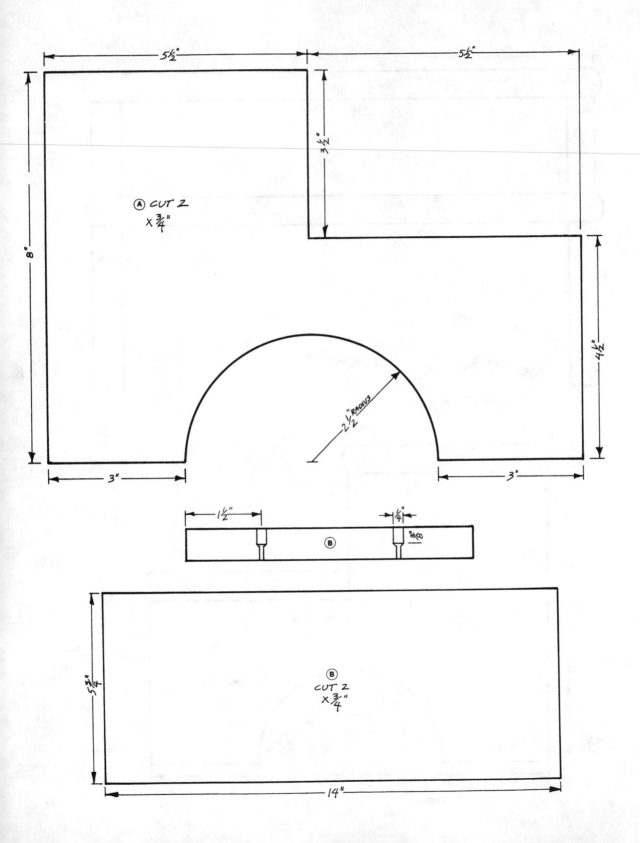

Old hanging file.

Antique Pie Safe.

Reproduction office shelf.

Antique Wash Stand and Towel Rack, which is holding a quilt.

Reproduction Crock Stand and Settle.

Old Shaving Mirror. Note knobs and feet, which were changed in early 1900s.

Old Spice Cabinet.

Hanging Corner Cupboard and Side Table.

Furniture

THE FURNITURE PROJECTS in this section are derived from typical early-American country pieces. The originals usually are one-of-a-kind, and although similar items can be found in museums and in private collections, rarely is there an exact duplicate. Even when colonial craftsmen used patterns or copied an existing piece, they adapted the design to suit the available wood and their own tools and abilities. These unique adaptations are what gives antiques their special charm and make collecting them especially challenging.

I have a collection of plank-bottom chairs that I use as a set, even though no two are exactly the same. Each new addition makes the entire group more interesting.

It is important to remember that only the most prosperous of the early colonial homes would have contained as many pieces as are presented here. The home of the typical early settler had one or two rooms, a loft, and often a dirt floor. The furnishings were few: a bed, a table, a bench, and a crock stand, for example. As the settlements grew and families prospered, rooms were added, ceilings and floors were installed, and more furnishings were bought or made. Of course, prosperous citizens in larger settlements had more substantial homes, which were sometimes furnished with imported items, but homes such as these were not common in the seventeenth century.

Many of the antiques featured here might have been crafted by a homeowner for his family's use. Others, such as the pie safe, were probably made by professional cabinetmakers who traveled from settlement to settlement making furniture to order.

The colonial country-style furniture shown in this book was built throughout the original 13 colonies up until the mid-1800s. After that time, factory-produced furniture became available, and the elaborate Victorian style emerged as the popular new fashion.

For a long period, the art of handcrafting wood nearly disappeared, but after the second World War, handwork and the functional designs became increasingly appreciated. Today, talented artisans in many sections of our country are reviving old methods and patterns. Early-American-style furniture, correctly made, is not only practical and attractive, but it also brings us close to the early settlers and to the history of America.

Whether you purchase originals or make reproductions using these patterns, you will enjoy living with part of our heritage.

Crock stand

FROM RURAL NEW YORK comes this reproduction of an antique crock stand. Similar stands were made in Pennsylvania, Maryland, and Virginia. Some stands are wider and shorter, but I prefer this rather slender, tall one. This stand has a diagonal brace inset into the back of the shelves, which makes it very stable. The rest of the construction is mortise-and-tenon, with dovetailing holding the top shelf to the sides. Make one of these for your kitchen or family room and display a collection of crocks or bowls.

Crock stand 63

Materials	Wood	
	2 pieces sides (A)	¾ × 9¼ × 47
	2 pieces top shelf (B)	¾ × 5 × 36
	2 pieces shelves (C)	¾ × 6¼ × 36
	1 piece middle shelf (D)	¾ × 7¾ × 36
	1 piece bottom shelf (E)	¾ × 9¼ × 36
	1 piece brace (F)	½ × 2 × 54

(Trim off excess after nailing onto sides and shelves.)

Miscellaneous
Glue
Sandpaper
1¼" finishing nails
Varnish or paint

Any colonial color is suitable for painting a stand like this. The antique one I copied was a soft gold, but use a color to complement your antiques. This project would look good antiqued or sponge-painted or even varnished. Decorate it to suit your decor and enjoy.

The measurements given here are for outside finished dimensions of blanks. Allow extra for tenons and trim off after making the stand. Use pine or poplar. The wood you choose can have firm knots, but be sure they will not be where you want to place a mortise, tenon, or dovetail.

Construction

1. After you have studied the working drawing and the plan on page 63, cut out all blanks, allowing extra for the tenons.

2. Cut mortises and dovetails in sides A. I like to cut completely around edges with a chisel after marking with a pencil. This sometimes keeps the wood from splintering around the edges. Trim out mortises and sand them smooth.

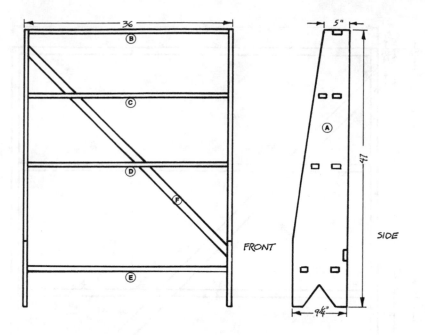

FRONT

SIDE

3. Mark the actual dimensions for tenons by placing the ends of the shelves next to the side mortises, using knife for marking. Adjust the pattern as needed. Cut out the tenons a little larger and longer than needed; then cut and trim them to fit neatly into the mortises.

4. Cut dovetails in the top shelf by marking from side, cutting slightly large, and trimming down as in step 3.

5. Assemble the stand. When all fits well, take it apart. Then glue it together, making sure it is all square.

6. Place the stand face-down. Place the brace across the back diagonally, as shown in the plan. Mark where the brace crosses the sides and shelves. Remove the brace, and cut the slots for it with a dovetail saw and chisel. Put the brace back in place after gluing the slots, and nail it in place.

7. Trim off any extra from the brace and tenons, and sand the project. Finish with paint or varnish.

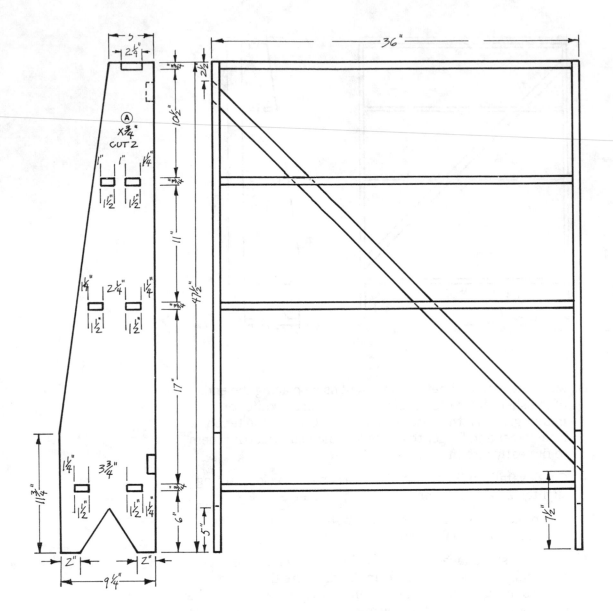

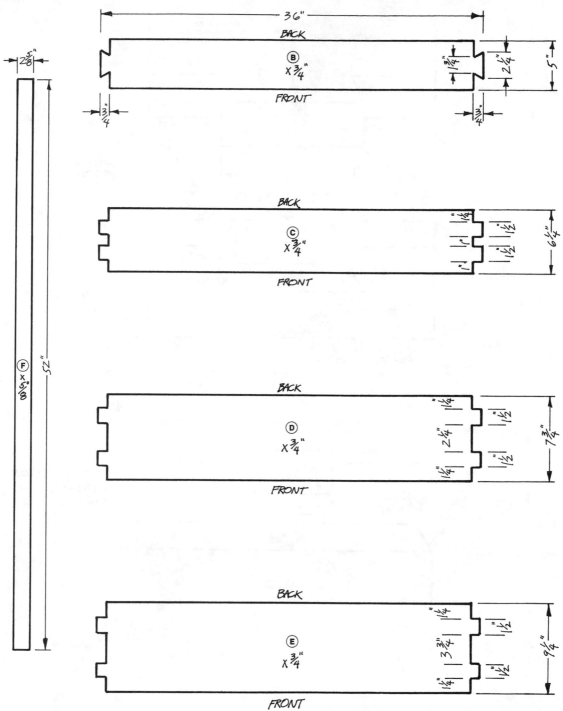

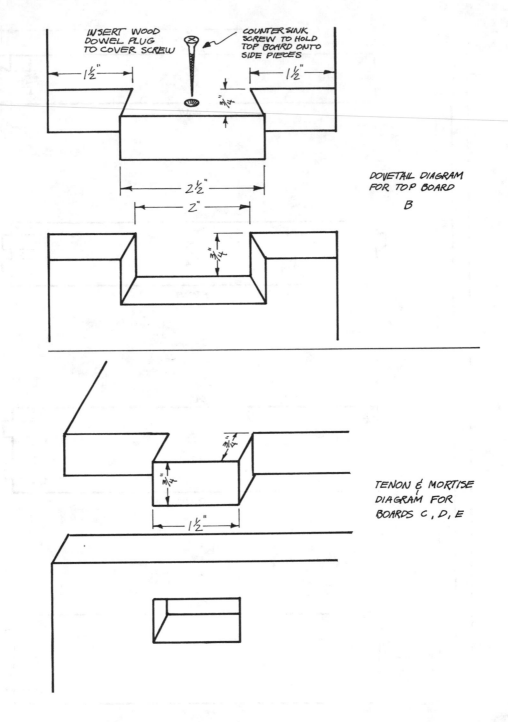

INSERT WOOD DOWEL PLUG TO COVER SCREW

COUNTER SINK SCREW TO HOLD TOP BOARD ONTO SIDE PIECES

$1\frac{1}{2}$"

$1\frac{1}{2}$"

$\frac{3}{4}$"

DOVETAIL DIAGRAM FOR TOP BOARD

B

$2\frac{1}{2}$"

2"

$\frac{3}{4}$"

TENON & MORTISE DIAGRAM FOR BOARDS C, D, E

$\frac{3}{4}$"

$\frac{3}{4}$"

$1\frac{1}{2}$"

Hanging corner cupboard

WHEN I FOUND THIS CUPBOARD at a Pennsylvania farm sale, its back was broken and chewed, and the rest was splattered with a heavy coat of paint and dirt. It now decorates a corner of my living room and is one of my favorite pieces. Beautifully crafted of cherry and walnut in front and poplar in back, it is lovely as well as useful.

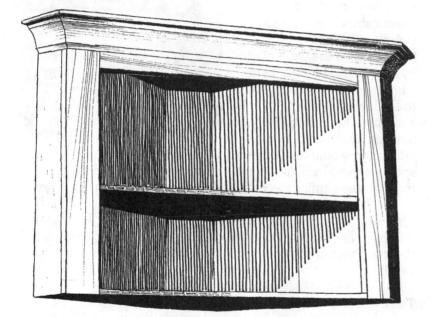

Materials

Wood

3 pieces (A)	⅞ × 16½ × 36
2 pieces (B)	⅞ × 3¼ × 26½
2 pieces (C)	⅞ × 3⅞ × 26½
1 piece (D)	⅞ × 4¼ × 27½
1 piece (F)	⅞ × 8 × 26½
2 sections sides (E)	⅞ × 22 × 26½

(These can be made of several boards ⅞"× 26½"of varying widths nailed to the shelves in order to fill in space.)
3"molding (G)   about 54 inches long, similar to pattern
1 section cap (H)   ⅜ × 6½ × 40

Miscellaneous
Old-style nails
Regular finishing nails
Glue
Sandpaper
Stain, wax, or varnish for outside

Hanging cupboards such as this one were rather common in the Pennsylvania-Maryland area. Originally, they did not have lower sections, although some have been joined with lower cabinets to make a complete cupboard. Sometimes these were made by itinerant cabinetmakers who traveled from settlement to settlement with their tools and drawings of furniture designs. These commercial craftsmen would take custom orders, which they made on the spot from local woods. These furniture makers account for many of the similar pieces found throughout the early colonies.

The antique I have was made with deep grooves in the shelves for displaying plates. The back can be painted blue or red, but the front should be waxed or finished with a clear matte varnish.

The measurements given here are for outside finished dimensions of blanks, and all dimensions are given in inches. For the front, sides, shelves, and moldings of the cabinet, use maple, cherry, or walnut, or a combination of these woods. For the sides, use any available wood.

Construction

1. Review the working drawing. Following the plan on page 71 and the pattern on page 72, cut out all blanks for As, Bs, Cs, and F, and sand them.

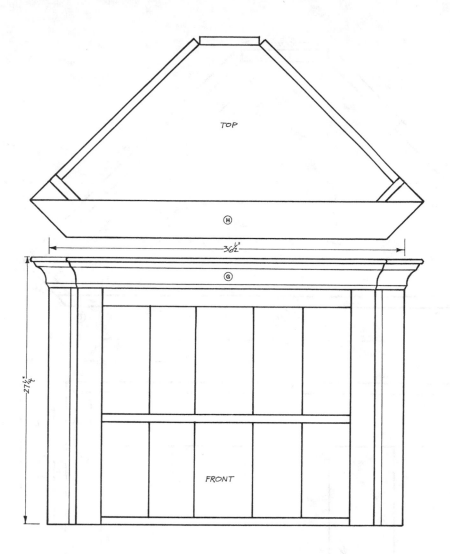

TOP

Ⓗ

36½"

Ⓖ

27¼"

FRONT

2. Rout or chisel grooves in 2 of As. (These grooves are for holding plates upright in the finished cupboard.)

3. Bevel the edges of Bs, C, and F. Cut mortises in the tops of the B pieces. Then assemble Bs, Cs, and F with As to make the basic cupboard shape. Measure and adjust the size of D to allow for tenons. Cut tenons, reassemble, and glue and nail together. Be sure to insert D into mortises in B and nail to top A. Sand and smooth all around.

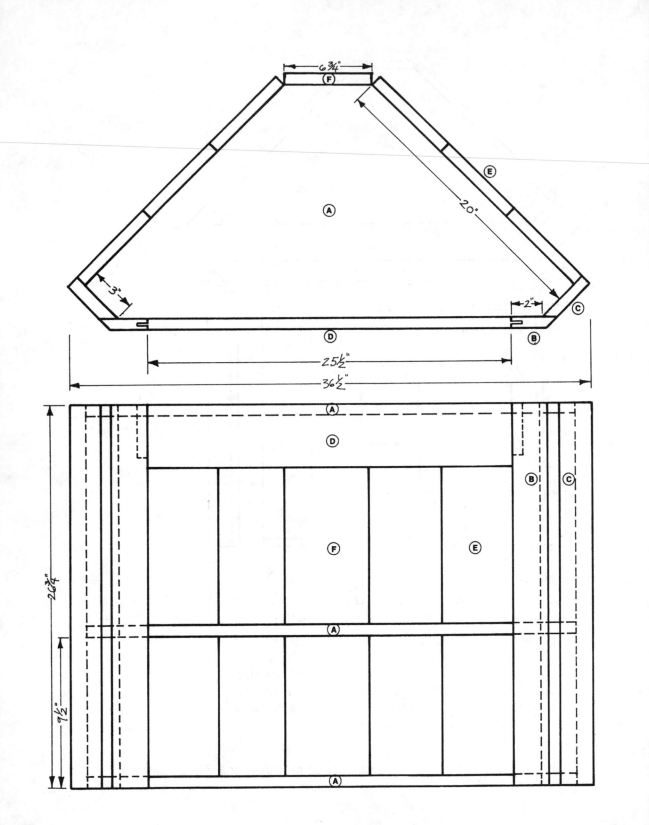

4. Nail boards to shelves to make Es. Use old-style nails for the front of the cupboard.

5. Miter the molding to fit around the top of the cupboard. Glue this together at joints, and nail in place, using finishing nails. Note that the molding extends down about 2" from the top.

6. Turn the assembly upside-down on blank for H. Draw a cutting line, allowing ½" extra at the front three edges. Round front three edges but stay flush at sides. Glue and nail in place to the top of the molding.

7. Stain or varnish the exterior of cupboard. An old-fashioned wax or turpentine finish is attractive if the woods are pretty.

8. Paint the interior with white, red, or a deep blue.

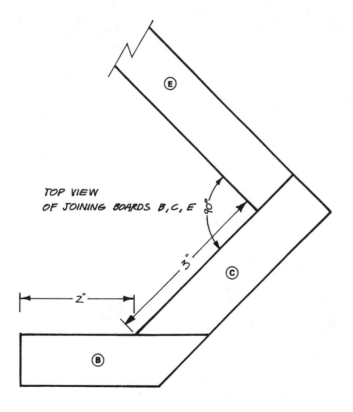

TOP VIEW
OF JOINING BOARDS B, C, E

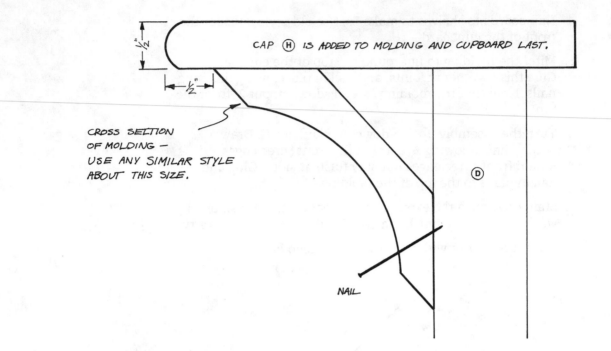

½"

½"

CAP Ⓗ IS ADDED TO MOLDING AND CUPBOARD LAST.

CROSS SECTION
OF MOLDING —
USE ANY SIMILAR STYLE
ABOUT THIS SIZE.

Ⓓ

NAIL

Pie safe

THIS PIE SAFE is from the
Delaware/Maryland/Virginia
coastal peninsula (which is
known locally as the Delmarva
Peninsula). The pie safe was a
very common and useful piece
of furniture in early colonial
homes. Used to store food,
especially baked goods, the
sides and fronts were fitted
with tin punched with small
holes in order to permit air to
flow back and forth without
allowing insects to get to the
food. The tins usually were
punched with geometric
patterns, but some old ones had
scenes or animal designs.
Patterns were punched either
from the inside or the outside,
depending on the look desired.

Materials

Wood for frame

1 piece top (A)	1 × 15 × 32	
4 pieces legs (B)	⅞ × 2⅝ × 54	
2 pieces top front & back (C)	⅞ × 2½ × 29½	
1 piece bottom (D)	⅞ × 2¾ × 29¼	
1 piece shelf (E)	⅞ × 14 × 28¼	
2 pieces shelves (F)	⅞ × 13⅛ × 28¼	
2 pieces curved (G)	⅞ × 2½ × 4½	
2 pieces top side (H)	⅞ × 4½ × 9¾	
(Includes ½" tenon on each end.)		
2 pieces middle side (I)	⅞ × 3 × 9¾	

(Includes ½" tenon on each end.)

2 pieces bottom side (J)	⅞ × 9⅝ × 9¾

(Includes ½" tenon on each end.)

2 pieces (K)	⅞ × 1 × 13⅛
Enough pieces to cover back piece (L)	½ × 41⅛

Wood for doors

4 pieces (a)	⅞ × 3 × 32
2 pieces (b)	⅞ × 2½ × 9
2 pieces (c)	⅞ × 3 × 9
2 pieces (d)	⅞ × 3½ × 9

Wood for drawer
(Pieces A through D can be poplar)

1 piece front (A)	1 × 4¾ × 28¼
1 piece back (B)	½ × 3¾ × 27¼
2 pieces sides (C)	¾ × 4½ × 12½
1 piece bottom (D)	½ × 12½ × 27¼

Miscellaneous
4 hinges for doors, brass or iron
4 hardwood knobs
8 pieces of tin or copper   9½ × 12½
Sandpaper
Glue
Screws and plugs or dowels
Assorted nails
Finishing coats and stain
Paint for interior

Pie safes were used in all sections of the colonies. Some, such as this one, had elaborately punched tins, while others had pieces of cloth stretched over the door openings. I have seen the legs of safes set in containers filled with water or oil to keep out crawling insects, but this could be a later development. In Pennsylvania, pie safes were sometimes suspended from the ceiling beams in order to prevent rats from intruding on the goodies.

The antique pie safe shown here is a very beautifully crafted piece, with the inner edges of the frames and the under side of the top beveled. The wood has a soft finish, probably wax and turpentine. In the original, all the tins are intact, but rats have chewed holes at the bottom front of the doors.

An odd feature of this pie safe is that the right-hand door is mounted upside-down and seems to have always been turned this way. Why the original maker did this, we'll never know. Perhaps he left the completion of the piece to an apprentice or son who made the mistake.

This pattern would look equally at home in a hall or dining room, but the antique is presently used in a formal dining room. You can add extra shelves if you like. This project will be a focal point for any decorating scheme. My own pie safe has coppered tins which, while it is not the authentic look, makes the safe very attractive.

The measurements given here are for outside finished
dimensions of blanks, and all dimensions are given in inches. I
recommend making the safe out of pine, cherry, or maple.
Make the drawer bottom and back from poplar or plywood.

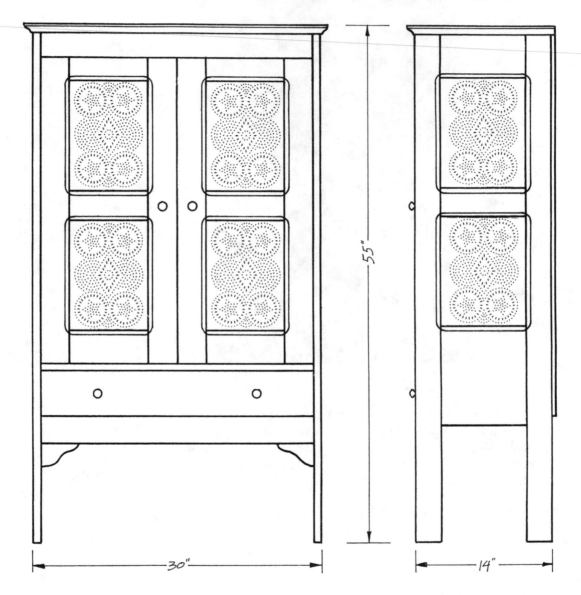

1. Trace or photocopy the pattern shown onto 12 sheets of paper. Tape the pattern to each of 12 sheets of metal; then tape the metal to a piece of scrap wood.

ENLARGE PATTERN TO 11" HIGH

2. Punch the entire pattern, using a flat-edge punch or a screwdriver for the lines and an awl or a metal punch for the holes. Practice on a scrap piece of metal until you are certain you are making the cuts correctly.

Construction of base

1. Following the patterns below and on page 81, cut all blanks and sand them. Cut ⁹⁄₁₆-inch-deep mortises in Bs to allow ¹⁄₁₆" clearance for tenons.

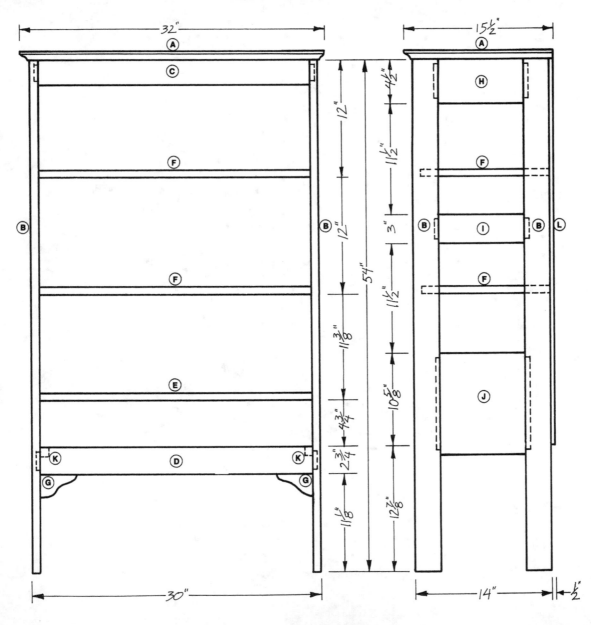

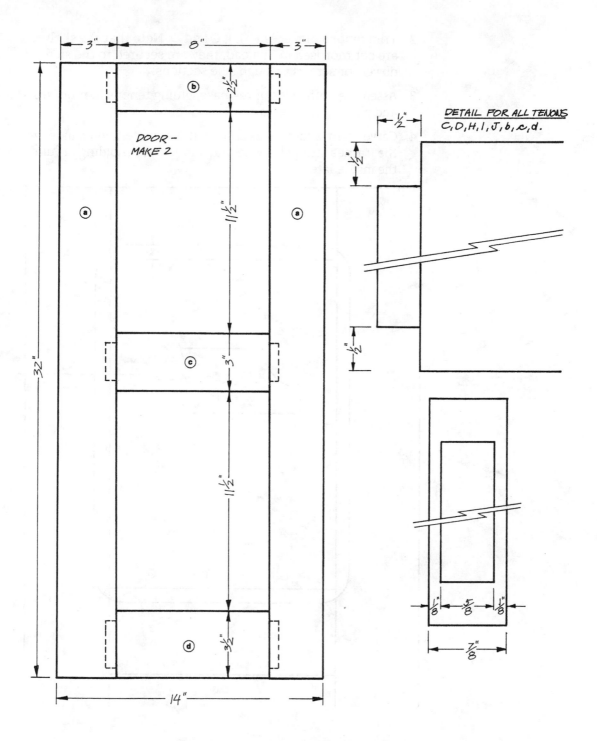

3" | 8" | 3"

b

2½"

DOOR –
MAKE 2

a   **a**

11½"

c

3"

11½"

d

3½"

32"

14"

DETAIL FOR ALL TENONS
C, D, H, I, J, b, c, d.

½"

½"

½"

½"

⅛"   ⅝"   ⅛"

⅞"

Pie safe 81

2. Trim tenons in pieces H, I, J, C and D. Note that the shelves are not mortised in. Instead, they are secured to the sides by dowels or screws through side sections.

3. Assemble both sides of the base, gluing tenons in mortises and pinning if necessary.

4. Carve frames for tins as shown. If you prefer, you can leave the frames straight-edged and add picture molding around the inside later.

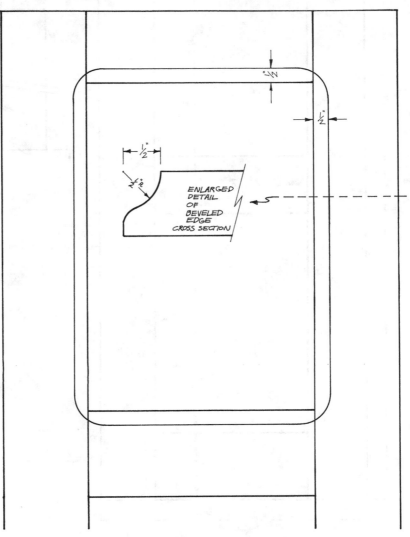

ENLARGED
DETAIL
OF
BEVELED
EDGE
CROSS SECTION

5. Fasten the tins in place in the sides. You must do this at this stage because the shelves will fit over them.

6. Glue and dowel in place first pieces C and D, then pieces F and E.

7. Shape the top around three edges as shown, and fasten it in place with glue and dowels and screws and plugs.

8. Screw and glue the K pieces in place. Cut out the G pieces using the grid provided, and glue the Gs in place.

9. Nail the back L piece in place. (If you prefer, you can postpone this step until the doors and tins are in place to allow access for assembly.)

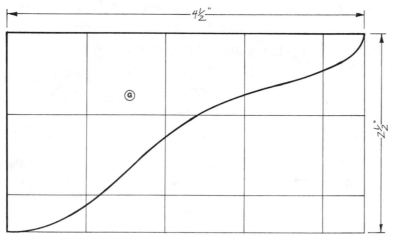

GRID SQUARES = 1"

Construction of doors

1. Again referring to the patterns on pages 80 and 81, cut out all blanks and sand them.

2. Cut ½" × ⅜" mortises in As. Make tenons on Bs, Cs, and Ds. When all fit neatly, take apart, glue, and reassemble.

3. Carve frames for tins as you did in sides of base.

4. Cut mortises for hinges in sides and on doors. Mount with hinges on doors. Then fasten the doors to the sides.

5. Glue E in place on one door.

Pie safe 83

6. Make a turnbuckle, and fasten it in place with a screw or nail.

7. Apply the final finishing coat to the piece. Then tack tins on the inside of the doors, centering each one.

Construction of drawer

1. Following the pattern shown here, cut blanks for the drawer, and sand them. Incise decorative grooves in A. Then cut a rabbet in the back of A, and rout a dado. Also cut dados in the C pieces.

2. Glue and nail the C pieces to the A piece. Slide bottom D in place.

3. Glue and nail B in place, and add small nails upward, through the bottom and into the back, to hold the bottom in place.

4. Add the knobs to the front of the drawer.

Finishing

Sand the entire pie safe with very fine sandpaper. Stain the piece, and add a finishing coat. The original is well-waxed to a soft sheen.

The original tins were left natural, but I like to copper my tins or use copper metal because it adds an interesting color. The inside of the original is unfinished. I like to paint the shelves and the inside of a pie safe with red or blue.

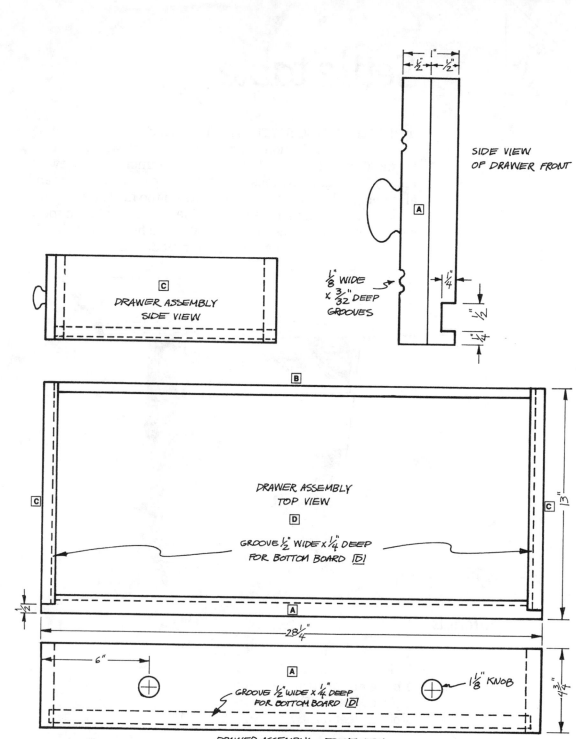

SIDE VIEW
OF DRAWER FRONT

A

⅛" WIDE
X 3/32" DEEP
GROOVES

¼"

½"

¼"

1"

½" ½"

C

DRAWER ASSEMBLY
SIDE VIEW

B

C

C

DRAWER ASSEMBLY
TOP VIEW

D

GROOVE ½" WIDE X ¼" DEEP
FOR BOTTOM BOARD D

13"

½"

A

28¼"

6"

A

GROOVE ½" WIDE X ¼" DEEP
FOR BOTTOM BOARD D

1⅛" KNOB

4¾"

DRAWER ASSEMBLY - FRONT VIEW

Settle table

THE INTERESTING SETTLE TABLE on which this project is based is in the collection at the Mystic Seaport Museum in Mystic, Connecticut. Settles were very common in the New England colonies. The tops were turned up to make a seat and also to provide protection from drafts on the neck. I think that they were just another creative double-purpose solution for early homes. When the housewife was finished baking she could turn the top of her table up and sit down.

Materials

Wood

2 pieces legs (A)	¾ × 12¾ × 27⅝
1 piece seat (B)	¾ × 10 × 17⅝
1 piece hinge plate (C)	¾ × 3 × 18½
1 piece bottom (D)	¾ × 11¼ × 17¾
4 pieces braces (E)	¾ × 1 × 11¼
2 pieces feet (F)	1½ × 2½ × 17¾

2 pieces aprons (G)   ¾ × 8   × 19¼
1 piece top (H)   ¾ × 23½ × 36½
  (Can be made from 2 or 3 boards 36½ inches long, joined.)
2 pieces brace (I)   ¾ × 3   × 21½

Miscellaneous

4⅝" round dowels for pins (J)
  (Or turn from 1 × 1 × 6⅛, following pattern)
Glue
Sandpaper
Screws and plugs for joining
Paint

Many settlers' homes used convertible furniture. For instance, tables and chests were used as sleeping accommodations in many small homes—and these might have been preferable to the beds that were filled with several people, who often had to sleep in shifts. This was a common practice even in the inns of the period.

The original antique is a very attractive design and small enough to fit well into a small room. I particularly like the design of the legs and the old red finish.

Antique on display at Mystic Seaport Museum, Mystic, CT.

I have a large settle table from New England that I use as a dining table. I use the box to store linens. When the table is not being used for dining, I turn the top up to provide extra seating.

Many of the antique settles have deep aprons, which make it difficult for tall people to sit comfortably while eating. Adjust the height and top width of this pattern to suit your family's needs.

The measurements given in the materials list are for outside finished dimensions of blanks, and all dimensions are given in inches. Use cherry, maple, pine, or poplar wood to make this project.

Construction

1. Study the plan and the plans on the following pages. Cut out all blanks.

2. Cut, assemble, and join the boards for top.

3. Rout or chisel dadoes and grooves in As and Gs. Cut mortises in Fs. Follow the patterns on pages 93 and 94 for this step. Sand all pieces, and drill holes in the top of A.

4. Glue and screw braces E onto inside of A pieces.

5. Assemble the base with all parts except the seat. Trim and fit where necessary until all fit neatly together.

6. Assemble with glue and countersunk screws where necessary to hold aprons G to the A pieces, and the F pieces to the A pieces. NOTE: Add back apron G last, after D and C are in place.

8. Round front of B seat. Trim and sand when it fits neatly onto box. Mount hinges on back edge and join them to C.

9. Place the top on the base assembly. Mark where the I pieces will fit, allowing ⅛" clearance between the I pieces and the A pieces to allow free movement.

10. Mark for placement, and join the I pieces temporarily to the underside of top H. Also mark the I pieces for drilling holes for pins; then drill the holes, and mount the I assembly on H.

11. Make pins, following the pattern on page 92.

12. Paint or varnish settle and assemble.

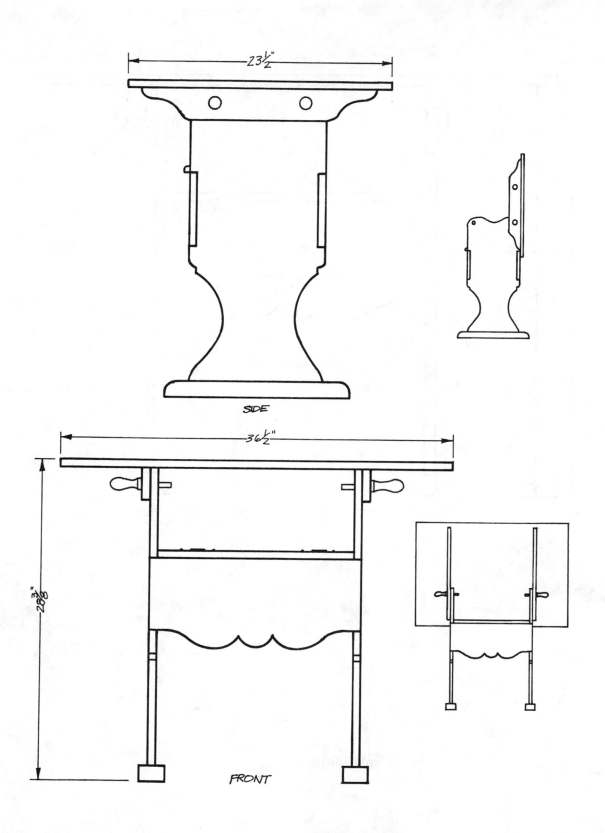

SIDE

FRONT

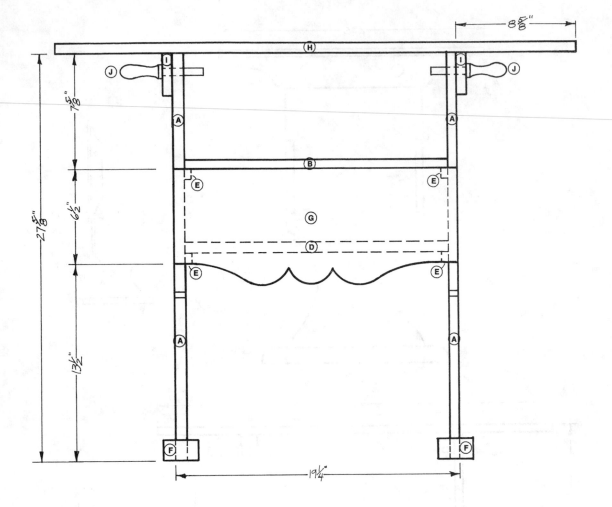

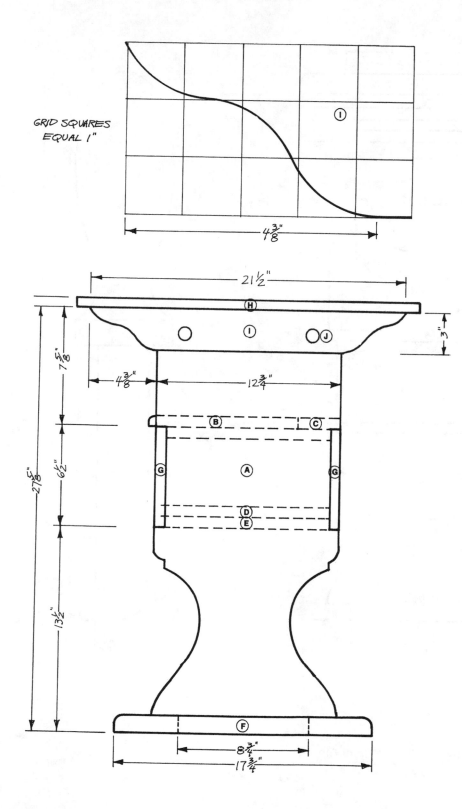

GRID SQUARES
EQUAL 1"

$4\frac{3}{8}$"

$21\frac{1}{2}$"

H

I

J

3"

$5\frac{7}{8}$"

$4\frac{3}{8}$"

$12\frac{3}{4}$"

B

C

$27\frac{5}{8}$"

$6\frac{1}{2}$"

G

A

G

D

E

$13\frac{1}{2}$"

F

$8\frac{3}{4}$"

$17\frac{3}{4}$"

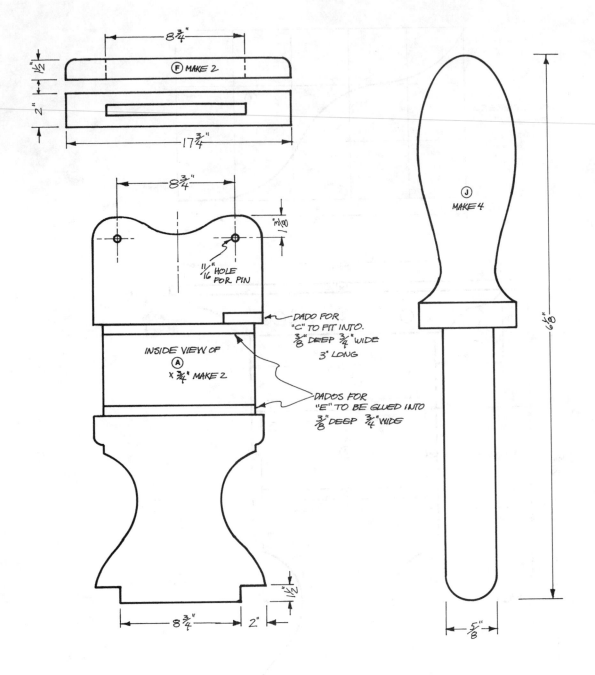

8¾"

½"

Ⓕ MAKE 2

2"

17¾"

8¾"

3/16"

11/16" HOLE
FOR PIN

DADO FOR
"C" TO FIT INTO.
⅜" DEEP ¾" WIDE
3" LONG

INSIDE VIEW OF
Ⓐ
X ¾" MAKE 2

DADOS FOR
"E" TO BE GLUED INTO
⅜" DEEP ¾" WIDE

8¾"

2"

½"

Ⓙ
MAKE 4

6⅞"

5⅛"

92 Colonial Classics

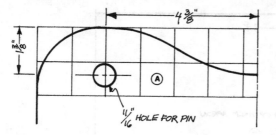

UPPER PART OF "A"

$\frac{11}{16}$" HOLE FOR PIN

GRID SQUARES = 1"

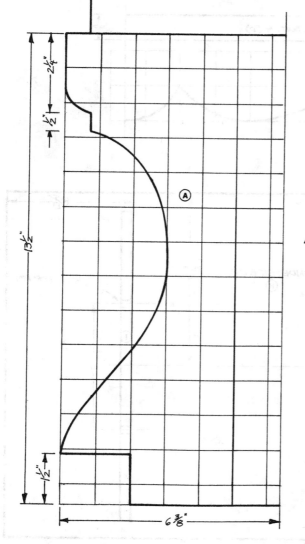

LOWER PART OF "A"

Settle table 93

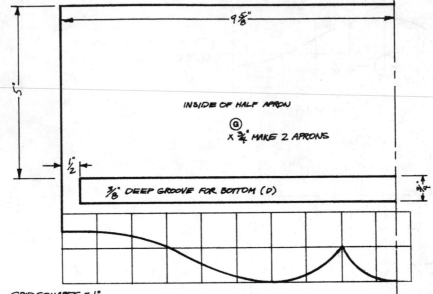

9⅝"

5"

INSIDE OF HALF APRON

Ⓖ

x ¾" MAKE 2 APRONS

½"

⅜" DEEP GROOVE FOR BOTTOM (D)

¾"

GRID SQUARES = 1"

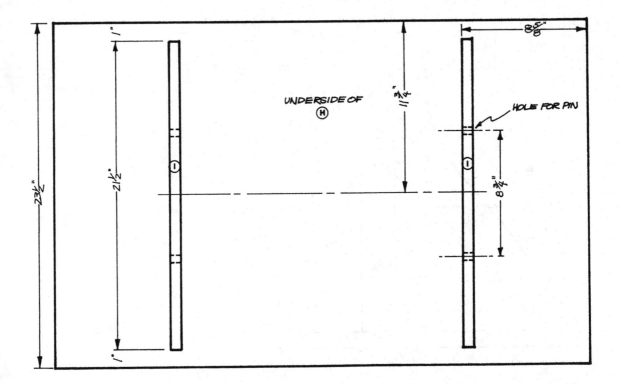

8⅝"

1"

UNDERSIDE OF

Ⓗ

1¼"

¾"

HOLE FOR PIN

Ⓘ

Ⓘ

8¾"

23½"

21½"

1"

Rustic bench

THE LITTLE BENCH SHOWN HERE originated in Virginia and is typical of the utility benches used in country homesteads throughout the colonies. They were used for working and casual seating, and they were often made to fill a specific need. The antique from which this pattern came has marks on the top where different tools were fastened over the years. The last one was a type of sausage-stuffer.

Materials

Wood
1 piece top (A)   ¾ × 9   × 42
2 pieces braces (B)   1½ × 2   × 9
4 pieces legs (C)   1½ × 1½ × 18½

Miscellaneous
4 wedges for top of legs
Nails or screws (1¾" or 2") for fastening braces to top
Glue
Sandpaper
Clear finishing coat to protect against weather and wear

Benches of this type were sturdily made and lasted through generations of hard and constant use. This one, though rustic, has been made with careful attention to design and detail. The legs are particularly interesting, since they are shaped octagonally for most of their length, with the top section rounded and tapered. Obviously the man who made this piece was proud of his ability and took care in crafting even this utilitarian piece.

Virginia has many museums of plantations and restored towns where you can see how early settlers lived and made their living. If you look, you will see benches similar to this one in almost every farm or shop.

The measurements given in the materials list are for outside finished dimensions of blanks, and all dimensions are given in inches. I recommend using a hardwood for the legs and braces of this stool, and pine for its top.

Construction

1. Begin by studying the working drawing and the plan to see how the project fits together. Following the pattern, cut out all the blanks for the top and braces. Sand these pieces.

2. Nail or screw the braces to the top.

3. Drill 1⅛" holes through the braces and the top, as shown in the pattern. Taper these slightly, from 1½" at lower edge to 1⅛" at the top.

4. Cut out the legs. Taper for the top 4", from 1½" diameter at the bottom of the round section to 1⅛" at top.

5. Below the round section at the top, cut the octagonal pattern with a plane. These cuts will make a roughly octagonal pattern. Do not be concerned if they are not precise. Sand well.

6. Insert legs through the braces and top, and wedge. Note that the legs extend through the top and stick up about ½" or more. Cut off the tops of the legs so they all are about the same height above the top. Trim the bottom of the legs so the bench stands squarely.

7. Apply a finishing coat.

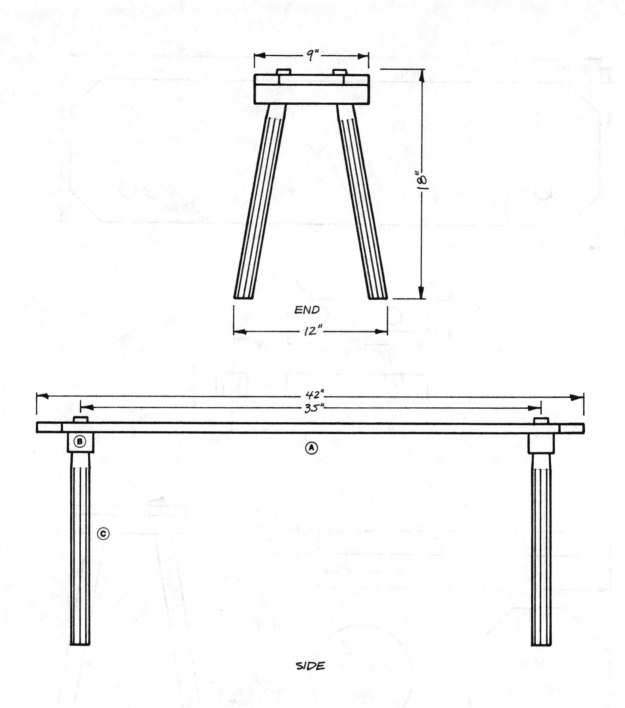

9"

18"

END

12"

42"

35"

Ⓑ

Ⓐ

Ⓒ

SIDE

Rustic bench 97

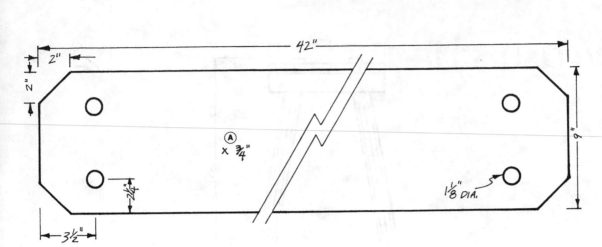

42"

2"

2"

9"

A
x 3/4"

1 1/8" DIA.

2 1/4"

3 1/2"

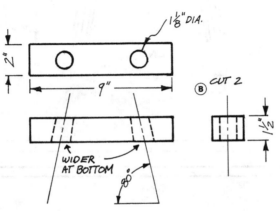

1 1/8" DIA.

2"

9"

B   CUT 2

1/2"

WIDER
AT BOTTOM

80°

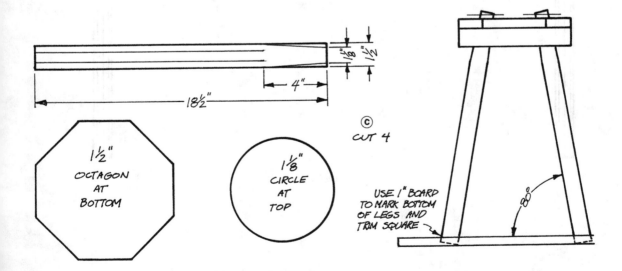

1/8"   1/2"

4"

18 1/2"

C
CUT 4

1 1/2"
OCTAGON
AT
BOTTOM

1 1/8"
CIRCLE
AT
TOP

80°

USE 1" BOARD
TO MARK BOTTOM
OF LEGS AND
TRIM SQUARE

Wash stand

THIS OLD WASH STAND from New
Hampshire has been in my family for as long
as I can remember. The hole in the top still
holds a china basin, the shelf below holds the
matching pitcher, and the drawer was handy
for soap and washcloth. These wash stands
were the only convenient arrangement for
washing inside when it was too cold to go
outside to the pump.

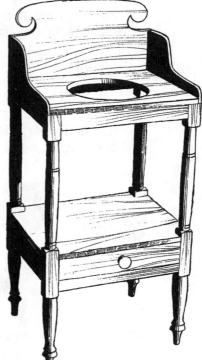

Materials

Wood

1 piece top back (A)	⅜ × 9¼ × 17
2 pieces sides (B)	⅜ × 5¼ × 14
1 piece base w/hole (C)	½ × 13⅝ × 16¼
2 pieces side base (D)	¾ × 1¾ × 11¾
2 pieces front base (E)	¾ × 1¾ × 14¾
2 pieces drawer (F)	¾ × 3 × 11¾
1 piece drawer front (H)	¾ × 3 × 14¾
2 pieces drawer runner (I)	½ × ¾ × 12
1 piece drawer base (J)	¾ × 1¼ × 14¾
4 pieces legs (K)	1½ × 1½ × 29¼
1 piece drawer top (L)	½ × 14 × 17
1 piece drawer front (M)	¾ × 3½ × 14
1 piece drawer back (N)	⅜ × 1¾ × 14
2 pieces drawer sides (O)	⅜ × 2⅜ × 10⅜
1 piece drawer bottom (P)	⅜ × 10 × 13⅜

Miscellaneous
1 wooden knob, 1½" diameter
Glue
Sandpaper
Screws and nails
Plugs to cover above
Paint, stain, or varnish

I particularly like the curves in the back and sides of this design. Many old wash stands have had parts replaced or have had solid tops added for holding a lamp instead of a bowl. This one is still as it was originally made. It has always been blue, as the many coats of paint revealed when a leg was scratched. I keep the old bowl and pitcher on top filled with flowers. If you prefer a solid top, just eliminate the hole for the bowl.

The measurements given are for outside finished dimensions of blanks. Use hardwood for the legs and for other parts that will show. The drawer back, bottom, and sides can be pine or poplar.

1. Before you begin, study the working drawing, the plan, and all the patterns on the following pages. Cut out all blanks and sand them.

Construction of main base

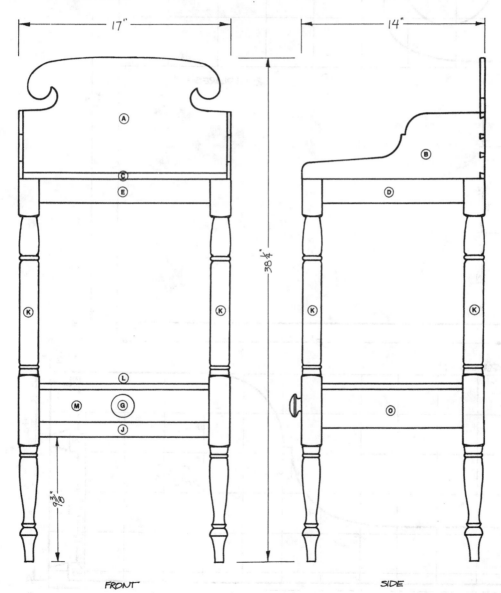

FRONT   SIDE

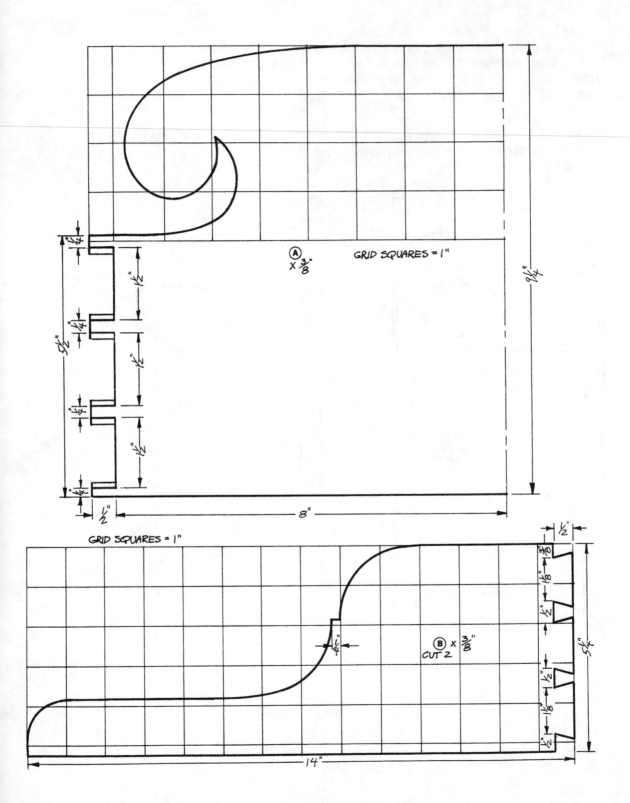

GRID SQUARES = 1"

(A) X 3/8"

GRID SQUARES = 1"

(B) X 3/8"
CUT 2

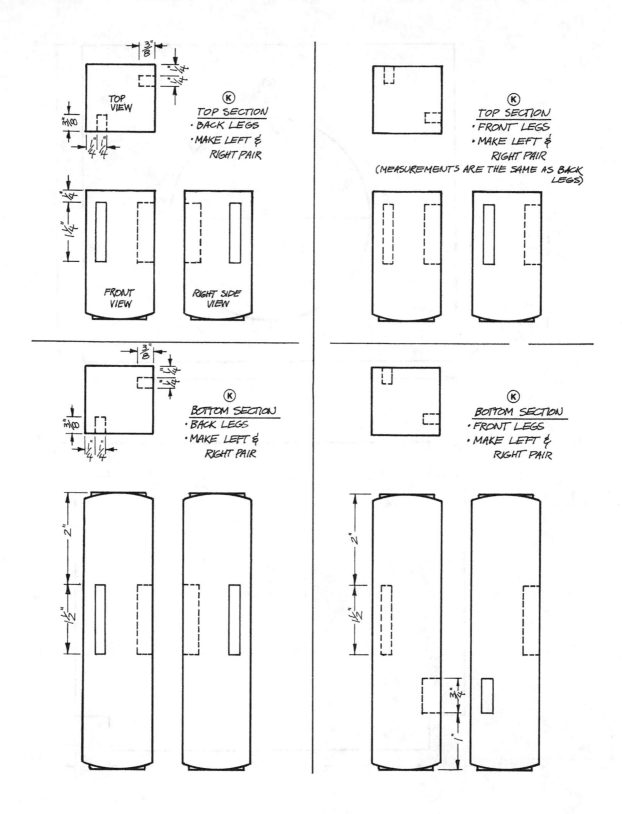

TOP SECTION
- BACK LEGS
- MAKE LEFT & RIGHT PAIR

TOP SECTION
- FRONT LEGS
- MAKE LEFT & RIGHT PAIR

(MEASUREMENTS ARE THE SAME AS BACK LEGS)

TOP VIEW

FRONT VIEW

RIGHT SIDE VIEW

BOTTOM SECTION
- BACK LEGS
- MAKE LEFT & RIGHT PAIR

BOTTOM SECTION
- FRONT LEGS
- MAKE LEFT & RIGHT PAIR

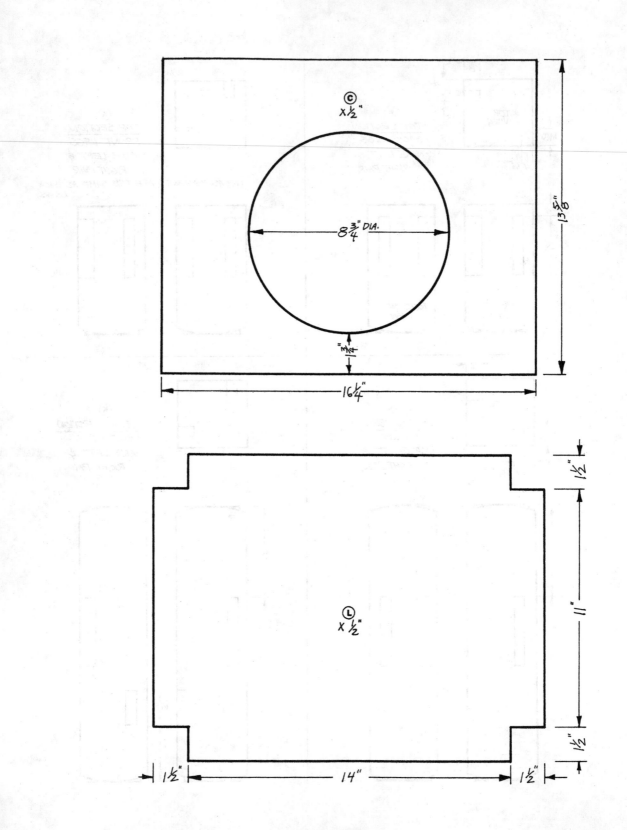

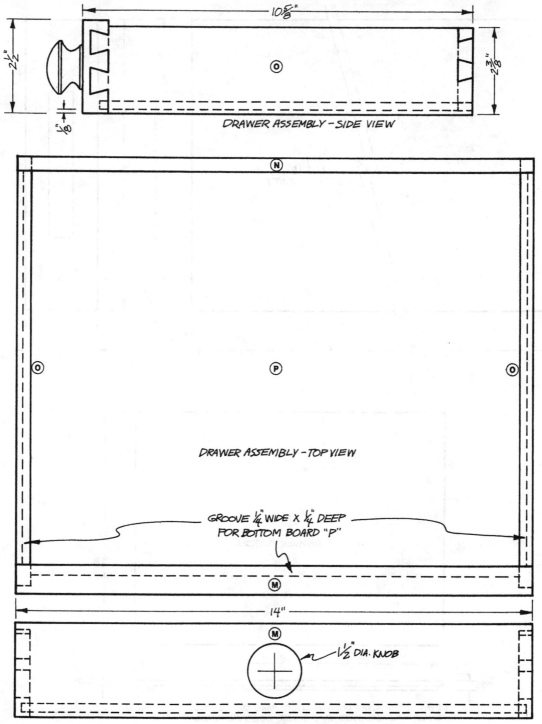

DRAWER ASSEMBLY – SIDE VIEW

DRAWER ASSEMBLY – TOP VIEW

GROOVE ¼" WIDE X ¼" DEEP
FOR BOTTOM BOARD "P"

DRAWER ASSEMBLY – FRONT VIEW

1½" DIA. KNOB

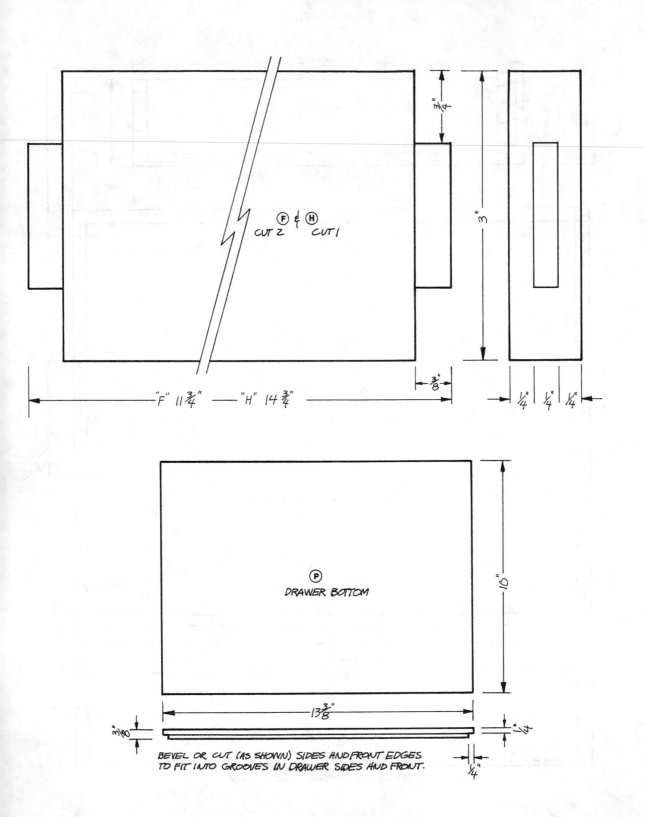

$\frac{3}{4}$"

3"

"F" 11$\frac{3}{4}$" — "H" 14$\frac{3}{4}$"

$\frac{3}{8}$"

$\frac{1}{4}$" $\frac{1}{4}$" $\frac{1}{4}$"

Ⓕ & Ⓗ
CUT 2   CUT 1

Ⓟ
DRAWER BOTTOM

10"

13$\frac{3}{8}$"

$\frac{3}{16}$"

$\frac{1}{4}$"

$\frac{1}{4}$"

BEVEL OR CUT (AS SHOWN) SIDES AND FRONT EDGES
TO FIT INTO GROOVES IN DRAWER SIDES AND FRONT.

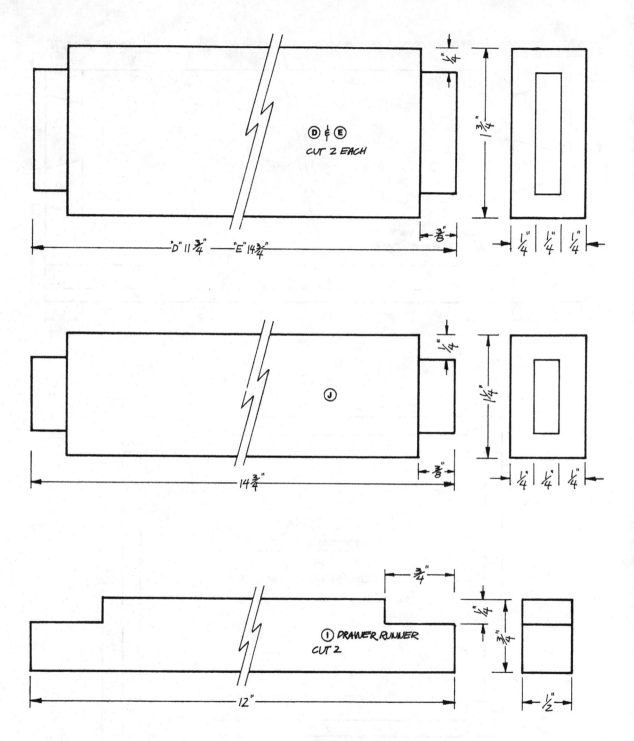

D & E
CUT 2 EACH

"D" 11¾" — "E" 14¾"

¼"

3¼"

⅜"

¼" | ¼" | ¼"

J

¼"

1¼"

14¾"

⅜"

¼" | ¼" | ¼"

① DRAWER RUNNER
CUT 2

¾"

¼"

3¼"

12"

½"

Wash stand 107

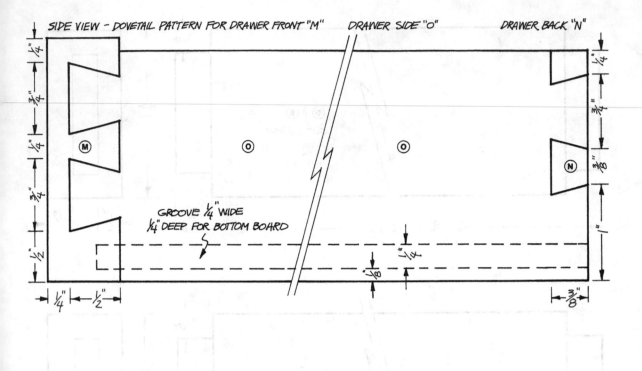

SIDE VIEW – DOVETAIL PATTERN FOR DRAWER FRONT "M"   DRAWER SIDE "O"   DRAWER BACK "N"

¼"

3"/4

¼"

M   O   O   N

3"/8

3"/4

3"/4

GROOVE ¼" WIDE
¼" DEEP FOR BOTTOM BOARD

½"

1"

¼" ½"   ¹⁄₁₆" ¹⁄₁₆"   3"/8

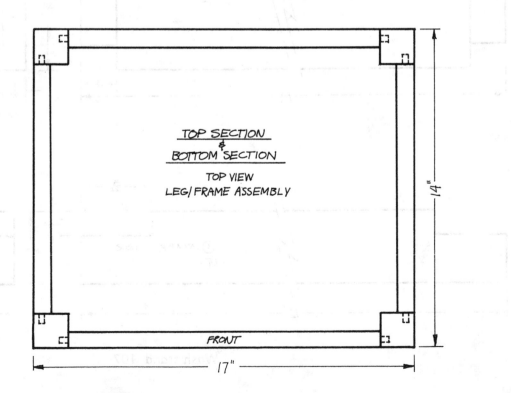

TOP SECTION
&
BOTTOM SECTION

TOP VIEW
LEG/FRAME ASSEMBLY

14"

FRONT

17"

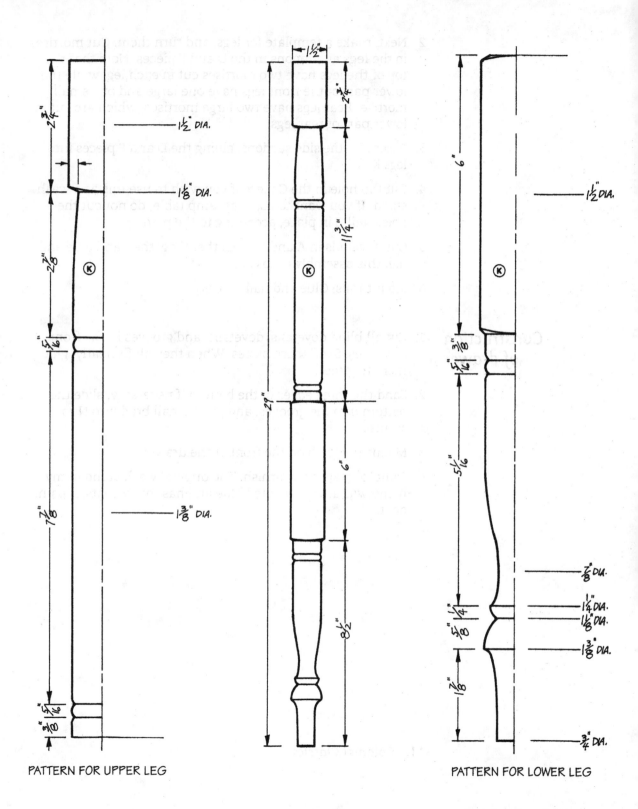

$1\frac{1}{2}''$ DIA.

$2\frac{3}{4}''$

$3''$

$1\frac{1}{8}''$ DIA.

$2\frac{7}{8}''$

Ⓚ

$\frac{5}{16}''$

$1\frac{3}{8}''$ DIA.

$7\frac{7}{8}''$

$\frac{5}{16}''$

$\frac{3}{8}''$

PATTERN FOR UPPER LEG

$1\frac{1}{2}''$

$2\frac{3}{4}''$

$1\frac{3}{4}''$

Ⓚ

$29''$

$6''$

$8\frac{1}{2}''$

$6''$

$1\frac{1}{2}''$ DIA.

Ⓚ

$\frac{3}{8}''$

$\frac{5}{16}''$

$5\frac{1}{16}''$

$\frac{7}{8}''$ DIA.

$1\frac{1}{4}''$ DIA.

$1\frac{1}{8}''$ DIA.

$\frac{1}{4}''$

$1\frac{3}{8}''$ DIA.

$\frac{5}{8}''$

$\frac{7}{8}''$

$\frac{3}{4}''$ DIA.

PATTERN FOR LOWER LEG

2. Next, make a template for legs, and turn them. Cut mortises in the legs and tenons in the D and F pieces. Note that the top of the legs have two mortises cut in each leg, while the lower part of the front legs have one large and one small mortise. Rear legs have two large mortises, which are cut in lower part of rear legs.

3. Assemble the side sections, gluing the D and F pieces into legs K.

4. Cut the hole in the C piece if you wish to use this as a wash stand. If you want to use it as lamp table, do not cut the hole. Nail C in place, according to the plans.

5. Cut dovetails in A and Bs. Join them together, and glue and nail this assembly onto C.

6. Mount rails. Glue and nail to legs.

Construction of drawer

1. Cut all blind dovetails, dovetails, and grooves in the front and sides. Sand these pieces. When they all fit neatly, glue them together.

2. Sand the three edges of the bottom if necessary, slide the bottom into the grooves, and put a small brad into N to secure.

3. Mount the knob on the front of the drawer.

4. Paint, or stain and varnish. The original wash stand in my home was always painted blue and has many coats of paint on it.

PROJECT 17

End table

THIS CHERRY END TABLE from Massachusetts has belonged to my family for many years. Tables similar in design to this one were made and used in many of the more substantial homes of the New England region, as well as in those of other coastal cities farther south. The legs, tops, and sides are usually of cherry, maple, or walnut; sometimes, all three are used in one piece. The unseen parts most often were poplar or pine wood. Typically, the legs are turned and joined by blind mortises and tenon, while the drawers are joined with dovetails.

Materials

Wood

Cherry or maple	
1 piece top (A)	¾ × 17½ × 21
1 piece (B)	⅞ × 4⅞ × 17
2 pieces (C)	⅞ × 4⅞ × 13½
2 pieces (D)	⅞ × 1⅜ × 17
1 piece (G)	¾ × 3⅛ × 16
4 pieces legs (L)	1¾ × 1¾ × 30¾
Pine or poplar	
2 pieces (E)	⅞ × 2 × 12½
2 pieces (F)	⅝ × ⅝ × 13⅞
2 pieces (H)	½ × 3⅛ × 13½
1 piece (J)	½ × 3⅛ × 16
1 piece (K)	⅜ × 13¼ × 15½

Miscellaneous
1¼" mahogany knob
Glue
Sandpaper
Nails, screws, and plugs
Wax or varnish finish
Stain, if needed to blend woods

These little tables were made individually, so even the most similar vary in some aspect, and each has its own special charm. I have several in my own home, but I am often tempted to acquire yet another one because of a special color or some interesting turning of its legs. Somehow, there always seems to be a corner just right for another small table. If you have a four-poster bed, you certainly will want one or two to place beside it. I enjoy having two in my living room, one in each hall, and some in the bedrooms. Make one or two, and you will have created a family heirloom to cherish and use.

Make the parts that will show from maple, cherry, or walnut (pieces A through L). Use poplar or pine for the rest of the pieces. The measurements given in the materials lists are for outside finished dimensions of blanks, and all measurements are given in inches.

Construction of base

1. Begin by studying the working drawing on page 111 and the plans. Following the patterns on the following pages, cut out all blanks for the body of the table and the top. Sand these pieces thoroughly.

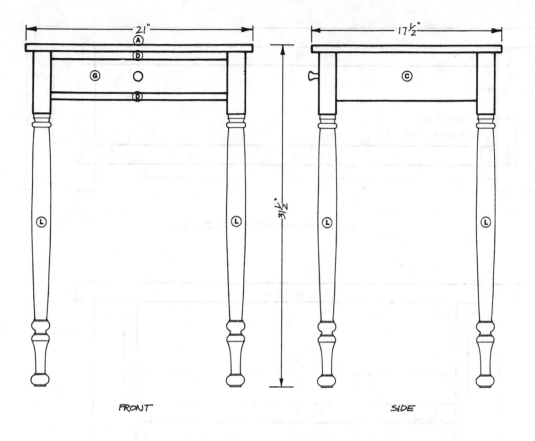

FRONT

SIDE

2. Make template for turning or carving legs, following the pattern on page 110. Allow extra wood at the ends of the legs, and trim them to size after turning and cutting mortises.

3. Turn legs following the pattern, and then cut mortises in top of legs. Note that back legs have different-size mortises than front legs. Cut tenons in pieces B, C, and D, and sand all parts smooth.

4. Assemble the side sections—one front and rear leg and side piece each. Glue together. Glue and screw E and F to Cs.

5. Glue B and Ds in place, completing the base assembly.

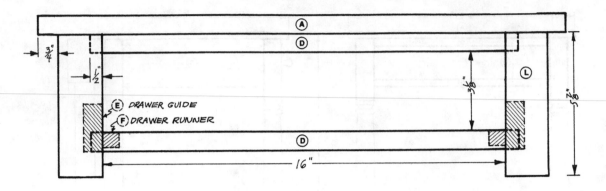

LEG/FRAME ASSEMBLY – FRONT VIEW

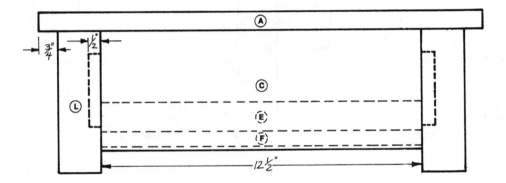

LEG/FRAME ASSEMBLY – SIDE VIEW

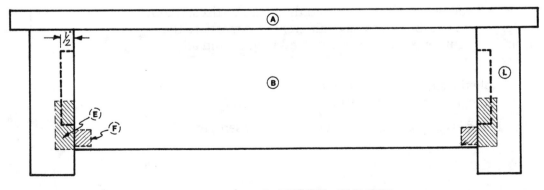

LEG/FRAME ASSEMBLY – BACK VIEW

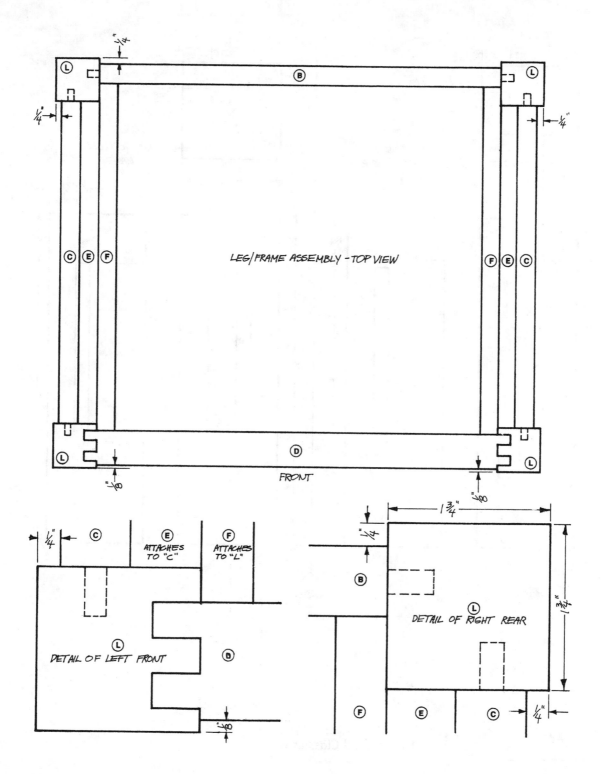

LEG/FRAME ASSEMBLY - TOP VIEW

FRONT

DETAIL OF LEFT FRONT

DETAIL OF RIGHT REAR

ATTACHES TO "C"

ATTACHES TO "L"

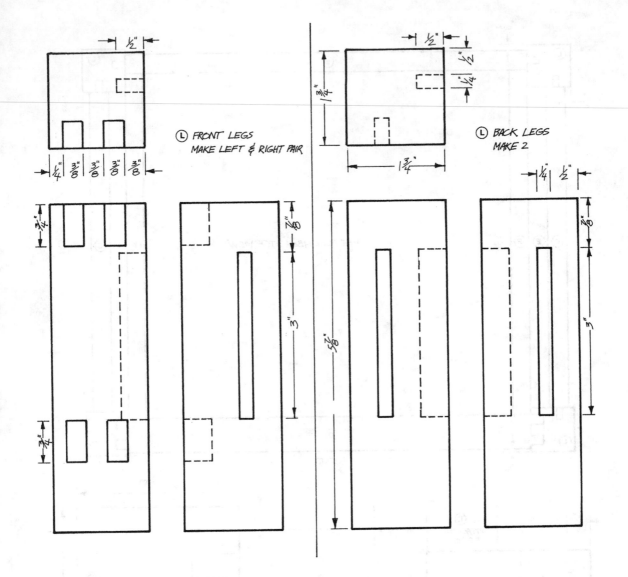

Ⓛ FRONT LEGS
MAKE LEFT & RIGHT PAIR

Ⓛ BACK LEGS
MAKE 2

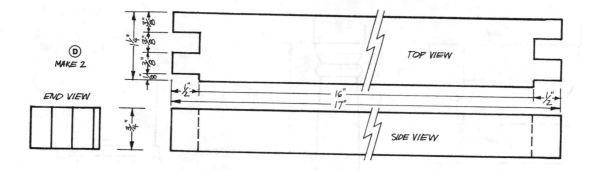

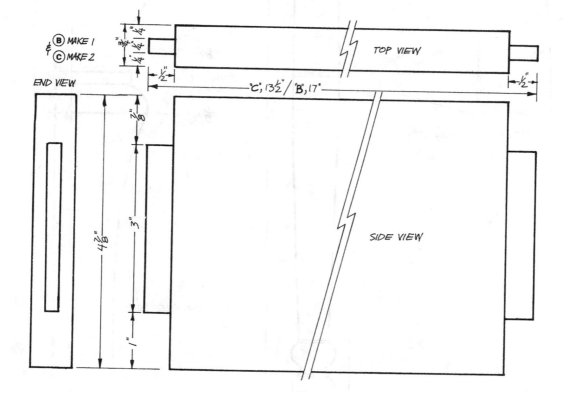

End table 117

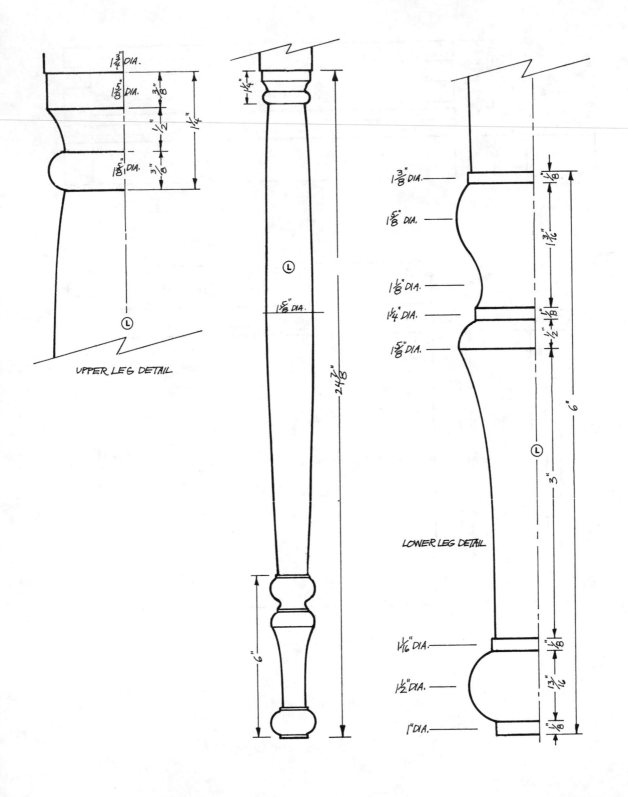

$1\frac{3}{4}$" DIA.

$1\frac{5}{8}$" DIA.

$\frac{3}{8}$"

$1\frac{1}{4}$"

$\frac{1}{2}$"

$1\frac{5}{8}$" DIA.

$\frac{3}{8}$"

L

UPPER LEG DETAIL

$1\frac{1}{4}$"

L

$1\frac{5}{8}$" DIA.

$24\frac{7}{8}$"

6"

$1\frac{3}{8}$" DIA.

$1\frac{5}{8}$" DIA.

$1\frac{1}{8}$" DIA.

$1\frac{1}{4}$" DIA.

$1\frac{5}{8}$" DIA.

$\frac{1}{8}$"

$1\frac{3}{16}$"

$\frac{1}{8}$"

$\frac{1}{2}$"

6"

3"

L

LOWER LEG DETAIL

$1\frac{1}{16}$" DIA.

$1\frac{1}{2}$" DIA.

1" DIA.

$\frac{1}{8}$"

$1\frac{3}{16}$"

$\frac{1}{8}$"

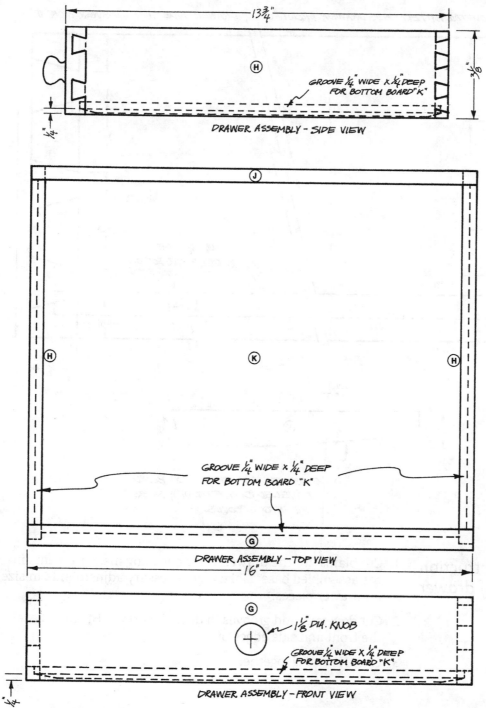

13¾"

3⅛"

Ⓗ

GROOVE ¼" WIDE X ¼" DEEP
FOR BOTTOM BOARD "K"

¼"

DRAWER ASSEMBLY - SIDE VIEW

Ⓙ

Ⓗ　　　　Ⓚ　　　　Ⓗ

GROOVE ¼" WIDE X ¼" DEEP
FOR BOTTOM BOARD "K"

Ⓖ

DRAWER ASSEMBLY - TOP VIEW

16"

Ⓖ

1⅛" DIA. KNOB

GROOVE ¼" WIDE X ¼" DEEP
FOR BOTTOM BOARD "K"

¼"

DRAWER ASSEMBLY - FRONT VIEW

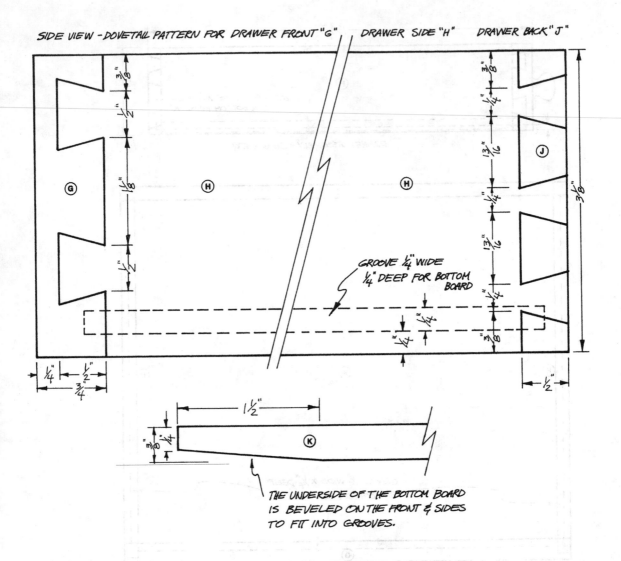

SIDE VIEW - DOVETAIL PATTERN FOR DRAWER FRONT "G"   DRAWER SIDE "H"   DRAWER BACK "J"

GROOVE ¼" WIDE
¼" DEEP FOR BOTTOM BOARD

THE UNDERSIDE OF THE BOTTOM BOARD
IS BEVELED ON THE FRONT & SIDES
TO FIT INTO GROOVES.

Construction of drawer

1. Cut blanks for the drawer, after checking measurements in the assembled base. Make any necessary adjustments in size for drawer pieces.

2. Cut dovetails and grooves in drawer parts G, H, and J. Bevel the front and side edges of K.

3. Glue Hs and G together.

120 Colonial Classics

4. Slide K into place, and then glue J in place. Nail the bottom of piece K into piece J.

5. Try the drawer in its space in the base. If necessary, add a drawer stop, gluing it to the underside of the top or to rails.

6. Attach the top using glue and nails, or by using screws angled upward, from the inside of sides C into top. Sand all over.

7. Fasten the knob to front of drawer. If you need to blend different woods together for a uniform color, stain the project. Then finish with varnish.